Five Minute Fast Fixes

Quick & easy ways to improve your health and wellbeing

Linda Hoyland, LMAR AKFRP

Five Minute Fast Fixes
Quick & easy ways to improve your health and wellbeing

ISBN: 978-1-8383170-0-3

Published by Linda Hoyland, April 2022

Disclaimer

The content of this book is for information purposes only and is not intended as medical advice, as a substitute for medical counselling, or a treatment/cure for any disease or health condition. It should not be construed as such. Always work with a qualified health professional before making any changes to your diet, prescription drug use, life style and exercise activities. The information in this book is provided as is, and the reader assumes all risks from the use or misuse of this information.

Contents

CONTENTS

The 26 High Touch Acupressure Points (APs)

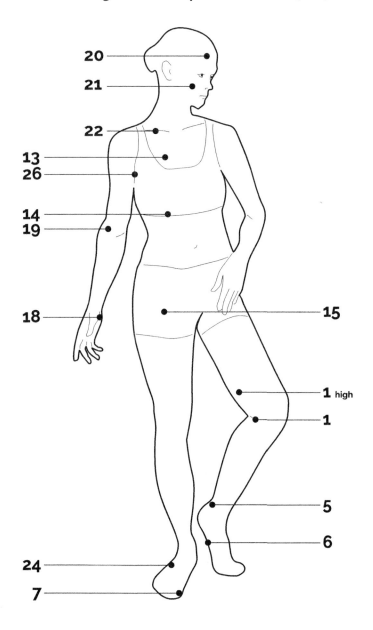

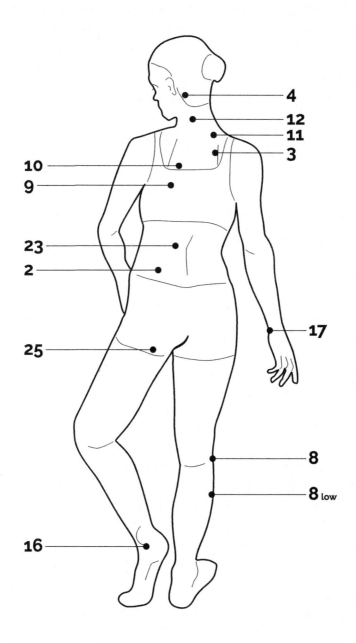

Acupressure Point locations:

AP1	is on the inside of the knee
AP2	is on top of the hipbone about 5cm either side of the spine
AP3	is on top of the scapula either side of the spine
AP4	is at the occipital area at the base of the head, either side of the spine
AP5	is on the inside of the ankle
AP6	is on the inside arch of the foot
AP7	is on the big toe
AP8	is behind the knees on the outside edge
AP9	is on the bottom tip of the scapula
AP10	is halfway up the shoulder blade on the spine side
AP11	is halfway between the base of the neck and the top of the shoulder blade
AP12	is on the middle of the neck at either side of the spine
AP13	is on the chest a few inches down from the collar bone either side of the sternum
AP14	is on the floating ribs below the nipple
AP15	is in the groin area midway between the pubic bone and outer edge of the hip
AP16	is on the outside of the ankle at the corner of the heel
AP17	is on the outside of the wrist in the hollow on the little finger side
AP18	is on the pad at the base of the thumb
AP19	is in the crease of the elbow
AP20	is on the forehead above the centre of the eyebrows
AP21	is just under the cheekbone in line with the eyeball
AP22	is in the hollow just under the collarbone next to the sternum
AP23	is on the back at the base of ribcage
AP24	is on the outer edge of the foot midway between the toes and ankle
AP25	is on the buttocks on your sitting bone
AP26	is at the back of the armpit

Five Minute Fast Fixes

Quick and easy ways to improve your health and wellbeing

Introduction

What can you do in 5 minutes?
- Run a mile
- Drive 6 miles
- Fly 45 miles
- Nap
- Experience a dream
- Load the washing machine
- Meditate
- Watch the ads on TV
- Have an argument
- Worry over something that may never happen....

We can use 5 minutes constructively, destructively or allow them to drift past us.

How about taking 5 of those minutes and using them positively to help ourselves.

Dipping into this book, deciding what is most important to you at this time and following the advice and tips is a way of giving you a quick power charge, specifically targeted to your concerns at that moment.

In just a few minutes, following the guidance here, massaging or holding the points indicated, the body responds with increased energy flow, followed over the next few days with a physiological response to the action. The blood and lymphatic flow improve, bringing oxygen and nutrients to the area of concern and removing the toxin build up in those areas, to be disposed of and eliminated from the body.

This means that those few minutes a day, will have a cumulative effect over time.

For example, from working on the knees one day, the effects will still be ongoing for the next day or so. If you continue to focus on this area everyday (and more than once a day), this can really help the healing process.

Of course, the body is not just a collection of parts; helping the knees will in turn create better posture, so helping to ease the back. Improving back problems will also have a beneficial effect on the knee joints too, as they will have to compensate less. You could then choose to focus on helping the lower back as well.

Another day, you may decide your aching shoulders need unburdening and because you have already started working with the lower back, the muscles easing in that area will be having a beneficial effect on all the back and shoulder muscles.

As the muscles realign themselves, the connective tissue within the body is eased off too. This tissue runs all through the body, connecting everything together, so again it will be helping the knees, lower back and even the shoulders before you have even started there.

What a fantastic piece of equipment the body is!

Test this for yourself:

Slowly bend forward, keeping your knees straight as if to touch your toes. See how far you can get without straining or causing pain anywhere. Straighten up and then put a golf ball (or you can use tin foil scrunched up firmly into a ball) on the floor and roll it around under the sole of your foot, making sure that it contacts all the parts of your foot, then repeat on the other foot. Now repeat the bending exercise and notice how much further you can move without straining.

Because you have massaged the connective tissue in your feet, this has a beneficial effect on all of the connective tissue within the body, indirectly helping muscles and joints to free up and relax, the result is increased mobility.

INTRODUCTION

This book is divided into health issues with fixes that will only take you a few minutes to do. It is designed to help you with every day health problems that can be caused by and interfere with, everyday life. It will give you strategies & exercises to help you feel better, physically, mentally and emotionally. An added benefit is that as one issue improves then other problems or worries will start to affect you less.

Everyone who reads this book will have a different reason for doing so.

Perhaps you were intrigued by the title, or maybe you've just started thinking about your own health care in a different way.

Someone may have bought it for you and you really don't have a clue what it's about.

You may have been seeing a complementary therapist and found it has really helped, so you are looking for extra ways to look after yourself.

Maybe you've been putting off seeing a complementary practitioner because you don't have the time or because you are not quite sure what it is all about. This is a really good way to dip your toe into the water and see if it is for you.

Whatever the reason, I hope you are inspired to read further and try out some of these techniques for yourself and discover how easy it can be to start improving your health.

Alternative/complementary medicine is actually meant to be preventative. Chinese doctors in the past were paid to keep you healthy, if you became ill, they weren't doing their job so consequently they wouldn't be paid.

At the end of the book you'll find a section on preventative health care, little things you can do to help yourself either daily, weekly or just when you feel like it, to remain healthy.

We have a lot to be thankful for now when it comes to our health. 200 years ago, we would have been lucky to reach the age of 30. We would have often been hungry and sanitation was so poor that infection was common and indeed often fatal. Also, childbirth could often be fatal for both mother and child. It does make you wonder how we have got to 2020, where more and more people are living into their nineties and beyond!

As well as sanitation, exercise, nutritious food and an active mind count for a lot.

In theory we are much more in control of our lives now—in practise we often have so much going on constantly that it feels as though that control has gone. We can spend so much time chasing about trying to achieve as much as possible, that our energy can drop just thinking about how much there is to do.

Anxiety and stress can be just as debilitating to our health as viral infections.

Scarily an international study[1] had revealed that a third of us have at least five ailments wrong with us (and that is over a wide age range, so not just as we get older).

Apparently less than 1 in 20 of us are completely healthy!

Use this book to help you become one of those who has good health!

Five Minute Fast Fixes is taken from my 30 years of experience as a complementary health practitioner. Having the knowledge and experience in reflexology, kinesiology, acupressure and nutrition, I know that it is best to have a full treatment as the body works as a whole. With kinesiology in particular, just one "fix" can do an awful lot of other problem solving too. Within a kinesiology session, time is spent using muscle response testing to determine which is the best solution for that person at that time given their personal set of circumstances. When that precise correction is applied then it can be like a domino effect, when one is pushed over it affects all the rest so it actually helps with other underlying and contributory factors too.

Because of this I have given as many solution choices as I can, then as you become more in tune with your body, you can gauge which one seems right for you, at that time. Each choice will have an effect, there will usually be one which brings about much more of a change. This will vary from person to person as everyone is unique.

Time factors will also influence your choice, massaging some points for literally 30 seconds may well appeal when you have nipped out of the office to the loo. Sat in the car in a traffic jam may give you more time to hold some acupressure points for a few minutes. Relaxing with a glass of wine in the evening or when having a hot bath, you may take the time to try out a longer treatment—the Main Central Vertical energy flow (see section on 'Preventative Health') or similar.

Some of these fixes will work almost instantly and others may need to be repeated often, depending on various factors. As a general rule, something that is very recent will go more quickly, given the right treatment. For example, if you have a headache caused by dehydration, then drinking water and rubbing the Kidney NLs (neurolymphatic points, see section on 'Headaches') will help pretty quickly.

Something longer term and more embedded will take more time (this is also where it becomes more beneficial to have a whole treatment), although being consistent will help enormously.

When working with a complementary practitioner they will use all their knowledge and experience to give you the best and most appropriate treatment for your health and wellbeing.

The kinesiologist uses muscle response testing to determine which protocols are priority for you at that time as well as those that will raise your vital force. Your body then makes the best changes with minimum effort.

A reflexologist will use their knowledge to understand what the reflexes are telling them and also help them decide which advanced techniques will help you best too.

Acupuncturists use pulse reading and other ways to find which meridians are out of balance and where to place the needles.

As you read through this book, you will be given quite a few options for certain problems and you may be confused as to which one to choose.

Which will be most beneficial for you?

* There are helpful comments with each one which will help you find the one that seems best for your particular problem

* You may be drawn to one option more than another, so follow your instinct

* You may have only a few minutes at that time so a shorter fix will appeal, you can repeat it as often as you think will help

* If you have more time available you can go for a technique that will take a little longer and again, you can use it later

* You can mix and match depending on time and inclination

The body will attempt to do its best with whatever you give it. Comparing the energy pathways of the meridians to the Underground system helps us understand that the acupressure points are a bit like the Metro stations which act as access points to connect us to those different levels.

Let's say you get on the tube at Kings Cross, there may be 2 or 3 different lines you can use to get to your destination. One will be the quickest, but the others will get you there too, it may take longer, it may be busier, there may be many more stops or changes, all of these making it more tiring, but you will get there. It's the same with the body, it may not be the precise fix the body wants, but it will do its best to work with what you give it. Similarly, using these techniques, some will work better for you than others. Because the body has taken some time to get to where it is now, it takes time for it to action the changes these techniques initiate, it also needs constant pushing to change its habits. A bit like the constant reminders the kids need to make their beds every day, eventually it becomes a new habit and part of their routine.

So although these techniques and exercises are quick and easy to do, to get the best results, they do need to be done frequently and consistently depending on how long you've had the condition and other health factors. You will notice benefits straight away with many of them though and definitely so if your ailment is more acute than chronic.

Quite often when we make the decision to change our lifestyle, it seems such a good idea, eat healthily, cut out junk food, drink more water, cut down on caffeine, go to the gym, cut out alcohol. But when you're already busy, finding the time to fit in the trips to the gym, the extra shopping that needs to be done, not to mention the time it takes to prepare healthy meals every day, it's no wonder people don't last the course.

It's much easier to make small gradual changes that are easy to keep up. And if you're wondering if small daily changes can have an impact, consider these 3 friends:

A decides to start going to the gym 3 times a week and cut back on cakes and biscuits.

B feels ok as they are and doesn't want to change anything.

C seems to spend more time than ever before watching TV and snacking a lot whilst doing so.

After a couple of weeks if you were to meet up with them, they would still look pretty much as they did when you last saw them.

After a couple of months, you might notice A looks brighter and has more energy, B looks the same and C is looking a bit bloated.

9 months later, B would look the same as before, C would have put on weight, look tired, have aching joints and probably feel quite unhealthy. Whereas A would look lighter, leaner, fitter and positively glowing with health!

All down to making small, gradual, easy to do changes to your everyday life.

Incorporating the techniques and exercises in this book into your daily routine will only take up a very small part of your day. These new habits will help your health now and also for the future. At the end of the book you will find a section on preventative health. As you become more in tune with your body and how to help decipher what it is telling you, you can use the information there to stay healthy for the future.

I had ulcerative colitis when I was pregnant and it was because of that, that I became interested in complementary health. Bear in mind that this was over 30 years ago and there wasn't much information available, reflexology for instance was pretty much unknown then.

Years later as my knowledge increased, I realised that I was suffering from candidiasis, caused by hormonal changes and indulging a craving for sugary foods!

Reflexology helped, as well as probiotics and I also began to understand that at the time I didn't tolerate bread very well. The episodes became less and also less fierce, but anxiety (and who doesn't have anxiety with young children!) made it worse.

I then discovered kinesiology, which literally stopped it overnight!

So, you can see that there were quite a few factors involved and contributing to the colitis. The point here is that these fixes will help a lot but changes to lifestyle habits, diet, etc will also play a large part in keeping your health in balance.

It's also worth focusing on what your expectation is when you use these fixes, as that can affect the outcome.

I had two clients with similar problems but different expectations and the results of their reflexology sessions were quite different.

The first client Mr M, arrived walking with a stick and a diagnosis of arthritis in his hips, the right one being the worst affected. He wanted to be free of the arthritis and able to walk easily again.

The other client Mr B had arthritis in his left hip and came to me so that he could play golf throughout the summer until he had a hip replacement.

After each session Mr M found his hips ached for a couple of days and then started to feel better. Mr B found that the pain in his left hip had gone halfway through the session and he would have 10 pain free days, playing golf before his next session.

Mr B had his hip operation which was successful. By the end of a year Mr M had pain free hips and an X-ray showed no signs of arthritis. They both had the same treatments, yet their responses were quite different and they both got their very different expectations met.

Take a look at the section on 'Hering's Law of Cure', for more information on how the body heals.

Over the years I have practised in complementary health care, there has been a big shift. At first clients would come to see me as they weren't getting satisfaction from conventional medicine and there seemed to be fewer chronic and diverse problems then.

There are more diagnostic methods and treatments available now, having different effects. So now when people decide to explore complementary health care, they will have been in the conventional system for longer, due to waiting times and more diagnostic techniques being carried out. Their illness has had more time to develop in the meantime, consequently their problems are more long standing and chronic. Now the complementary treatment has to do more and also work alongside their conventional treatment—which is of course why it is complementary.

However, these fast fixes will not only have an effect on the problem manifesting at the moment, but will as explained previously, carry on working and doing something to help longer standing problems.

Addendum

When I started writing this book a few years ago, I had all the ideas, but not enough time to actually write it. Quite ironic really when the book is all about quick and easy ways to improve your health when you don't have much spare time!

Our lives seem to be so frenetic, when you factor in family, work, social media pressures and demands that we are available virtually 24/7. Hence the title Five Minute Fast Fixes.

Because everyone can spare 5 minutes out of their busy day to fit in something to help them improve their health. Some of the techniques are shorter than 5 minutes and some take a bit longer. Those that take a bit longer can be done while you're watching TV, or lying in bed if you can't sleep, so there really is no excuse to not do them.

So, I was writing a book that I was too busy to spend much time on, for everyone who hasn't time to sort out their health niggles.

Then suddenly along came Covid-19! As I couldn't physically see clients, I was able to write more.

Having that time to spend writing has really worked out well, because the book is finished and it has been a joy to work on it.

About the Author

Linda Hoyland has been a complementary therapist for over 30 years now. Her career began as a chemist in Research and Development for the pharmaceutical industry. When pregnant, she became quite ill and the only thing offered were drugs, which as an expectant mum she really didn't want to take.

After having her son, she started Yoga classes and through these, went to a talk on Reflexology. As a scientist she was hugely sceptical yet intrigued, which led to her qualifying as a reflexologist.

Although loving working with reflexology clients and having amazing results, she realised that more could be done and so started looking for something else and eventually found the "holy grail" of therapies–kinesiology! Having trained with Terry Larder in Classical Kinesiology, she has also added other kinesiologies and High Touch Acupressure (Jin Shin) to her repertoire.

A member of the Association of Reflexologists and Federation of Kinesiologists, she was part of the KF Policy Board working on the Training Standards team for 6 years.

She was hugely fortunate to have brought up her children using just reflexology and kinesiology for their health whilst at home.

As a therapist for over 30 years Linda offers a truly holistic approach, looking at all aspects of a person's health, not only addressing structural, environmental and nutritional needs but also helping the release of emotional stress and limiting beliefs. She enjoys working with clients and loves seeing how much they benefit from the treatments in all sorts of ways.

Linda has seen many hundreds of clients regain their health and achieve their goals.

Many of them have used the techniques in this book with good results.

How to use the fixes

The chapters in this book relate to some of the more common problems that people have and are divided into 3 types of information.

Each chapter has some general information on the condition.

> The fast fixes are listed and appear in a tinted box like this one, they will also have a * next to each step, so you can easily follow them.

The information in italics gives a bit more detail about how best to use it or how it has helped others.

Depending on how much time you have, you can read all of the chapter or just go straight to the fast fixes and use those that fit your requirements the best.

There are charts so you can see where these contact points are. Most are on the same page as the exercises. The chart for the 26 High Touch Acupressure points (APs) that are used frequently, is at the front of the book.

Some of the fast fixes use neurolymphatic points (NLs) that will increase the lymph drainage to various areas of the body, relieving congestion and flushing out toxins from these areas. This allows more nutrients and oxygen to flow to those areas, so they feel less tense, less sore, move more freely, be more nourished and cleansed so consequently they will function more efficiently.

Other points are neurovascular points (NVs) which will increase the blood flow to those areas having a nourishing and cleansing effect too. These points were discovered in the 1930s by a Chiropractor who injected radioactive dye into people and monitored the blood flow to the organs whilst holding various points on the head. He found which points increased the blood flow to corresponding organs and so was able to map out all of the neurovascular points. Unfortunately, he died from radiation poisoning.

A lot of the fast fixes use acupressure points (APs) from the High Touch Acupressure (Jin Shin) system. These points are on a network of energy pathways around the body, the meridians. Meridians run along the surface of the body as well as at deeper levels, connecting energetically the organs that they are named after.

There has been a study[2] done using CT scans to detect acupuncture points in the body. The CT imaging shows clearly that there are structural differences with higher blood vessel concentration at the acupuncture points.

The researchers commented that other research has also found unique structures of acupuncture points and acupuncture meridians using MRI (magnetic resonance imaging), infrared imaging, LCD thermal photography, ultrasound and other CT imaging methods.

It is fascinating that science is now proving the existence of medicine that has been around for thousands of years!

Comparing the meridians to the Underground system helps us understand that the acupressure points are a bit like the Metro stations which act as access points to connect us to those different levels. These points allow the flow of energy from where there is excess to where there is not enough, removing blockages and congestion at these points, thereby energy can flow freely throughout the body. When the points are blocked, the energy flow stops or slows down. A blockage in the flow of energy results in an energy imbalance and can lead to discomfort on physical and emotional levels.

There are 26 of these acupressure energy points (APs) on both sides of the body.

Blockage at these points can lead to imbalance and eventually disease. When their energy flow is interrupted, then the points can become congested, the area can be sensitive or tender to the touch. Often there will be a sore spot there, showing that the point needs work. The area may also be bloated or puffy as the body tries to protect it, as it may be more vulnerable because of the blocked flow.

These points are simple and easy to use. We hold the points in conjunction with each other, gently touching and holding two points together at a time. The energy coming through our hands from the universe acts like a spark to the body's energy system, you can also compare it to jump leads starting a car when the battery is flat.

When the congested point is opened, then the energy can start to flow, cleansing and nourishing those areas.

We can also use more points in a sequence to create a flow of energy moving through the body to help with certain ailments.

You can see from the charts that the points are in precise areas, however the energy surrounding these points is of a similar size to a tennis ball, so as long as your fingers are covering that area you will be connecting with the point. You can either connect to the point by touching the skin or you can hold your hand an inch or two off the body in the energy field.

When using the acupressure points for specific issues that are only on one side of the body, for example a sore knee, then:

* If the problem, pain or inflammation is on the right side—treat the right side
* If the problem, pain or inflammation is on the left side— treat the left side
* If the problem is in the present, if you are aware of what may be causing it, or if a male energy is involved, then treat the right side
* If the problem is from the past, if you don't know why it has happened, or if a female energy is involved, then treat the left side
* You can use your intuition, whichever side you instinctively choose
* If in doubt do the right side first to clear the present, then the left to clear the past

Stress and anxiety

Stress can be good for us; the stress of a deadline pushes us to perform better and faster to get the result we want. This in turn gives us that feeling of achievement, releasing feel good hormones, which then allow us to reduce our pace back to our normal state—in an ideal world!

Nowadays we have constant stresses, constant deadlines, constantly having things on our mind that we need to do.

There is also stress on us from other aspects of living–poor nutrition, illness, family issues, injury and trauma to the body. If we are in balance, although these will have an impact on us, it is going to be less than if we are already stressed and under strain.

Our bodies are programmed to respond to a stressful event by producing adrenalin which prepares us to either stand and fight or take flight to remove ourselves from the stressful situation.

For instance, if someone at work takes us to task about our work (whether justified or not) our body will prepare us to "fight" without us even consciously thinking about our response. Although these days the "fight" may probably be verbal rather than physical! It may alternatively get us ready to take "flight" which could literally mean getting away from the situation—probably to the loo!

This "fight or flight" reaction is a survival response from years ago when our ancestors found themselves in a dangerous situation. If they were chased by some wild animal, they would run away as fast as they could, possibly clambering up a tree to get away. So, the next time something similar would happen, the thinking rational part of the brain is bypassed and they react from instinct, doing what they did before to get them out of the dangerous situation—even if the tree is a long way away—because that is what saved them the time before.

In childhood if someone tells us off, we may start crying and then be comforted because we are upset. This has then set up a response to criticism by crying, which in adulthood can be embarrassing in certain situations.

Our minds will often file events that are similar together, so anything that occurs that resonates with some part of that filing system could trigger a reaction. This may seem totally irrational and out of proportion to what has actually happened. In effect, we can become anxious for what appears to be no reason and has no obvious cause.

It's said that all illness has its roots in stress, or rather our reactions to stressors.

It's an indication that we cannot cope with the stressful demands on us. Stress in this case is not just work, relationship or other emotional stresses, but also the stresses on our body that can be caused by eating the wrong foods, a highly processed diet or not enough water. Today's sedentary lifestyle can put a strain on our bodies as well as RSI from computers, phones etc.

Injury or trauma to the body causes stress in other muscles and the organs, they all have to work harder to compensate for the other parts becoming faulty.

Emotional stresses are a drain on our adrenal glands, causing us to become tired all the time with no get up and go. Constant adrenal stimulation can also lead to fatigue, hormonal imbalances, anxiety, sleeplessness, heartburn and other problems.

After a stressful event the body returns the blood flow to the internal organs and directs it away from the brain and muscles so we feel shaky and spaced out. If there is constant stress, for instance continuous stressful situations at work or at home, long hours, tiredness, or not eating properly, the stress button is always being pressed so we never get a real chance to recover from the adrenalin overload. Hence, we can feel anxious, spaced out, fatigued and can't concentrate properly.

If we can reduce the effects that stress has on us, then we will have more energy, feel calmer, reduce the worry and sleep better.

Stress of this sort also affects our digestion, switching it off to allow us extra energy to deal with the problem at the time. This is one of the reasons why IBS is so prevalent these days. If our digestion is constantly affected, then we are not breaking down the food we eat into nutrients to fuel the body. If our body is not getting the right nutrients, it is going to function less efficiently. Think of a car, if you put the wrong fuel in, it may go but not for long! If you put the right fuel in but get the mixture of petrol: air wrong, then it has no power. It can chug along on the flat but ask it for any extra—to go up a hill or overtake at speed and it will let you down by being unable to perform.

The same with our bodies. As things deteriorate, we are able to manage everyday life (just) but cannot cope with extra demands on us. We snap at little things; it is usually the small extra stresses that cause the biggest (over) reaction. If we put the right fuel into our bodies, we have a better chance of having extra reserves of energy to cope with those extra demands on us.

If we can cope with these demands without depleting our reserves too much, then we are more likely to not react as much to stressful situations. This means we deplete ourselves less and actually start to build up our energy and vitality again.

Often as people start to get better, it is the small things they notice first. They feel less irritable in situations that before they would have blown their tops. They also find that they feel much less panicky and overwhelmed and more relaxed when faced with events they would previously have found very demanding.

Stress also shows itself in our posture, we can actually look tense, stiff and unrelaxed. Yoga, stretching exercises or relaxation techniques and meditation can all help to relax our posture. As can reflexology, massage and kinesiology. Cross-crawl can help to rebalance us too (see section on 'Dips in energy during the day').

Vitamin C and the B vitamins are helpful for protecting the body from the effects of stress.

We can hold a lot of stress in the jaw, which can lead to teeth grinding, headaches or neck tension. This can be reflected in our face in frown lines or lines around the mouth, so stress relieving techniques can help us look younger!

There are acupressure points on the face, which when pressed gently can help stimulate the blood flow to rebalance the underlying muscles and release the tension.

Just as stressful events and situations can cause us to feel tense, anxious or upset, and so disturb our body functions, then conversely pleasant situations and events have the potential to release tension and calm anxiety.

The sight of young children playing, a blue sky, the sun, a beautiful vista and picturesque view, a friendly conversation, a lovely meal. All of these things can restore balance and harmony to our body and soul. Sometimes we need to seek out pleasurable situations to change our perspective and move us out of a negative state.

Many lifestyle changes can be made to dissipate the stressful situations we may find ourselves in. And if they cannot be avoided, then these changes can at the very least help us deal with those stresses better.

Stress is a complex issue, so all of these suggestions will help in small yet significant ways.

FAST FIXES

If we can reduce the effects that stress has on us, then we will have more energy, feel calmer, reduce the worry and sleep better. This is a great technique to help reduce the effects of stress.

Many years ago, I had a client who was due to have some major dental work done which would take 4–5 hours. She was very worried about it for lots of reasons, as you can imagine. We used this method below, with her thinking about what she was fearful of, then she changed it to seeing herself sitting calmly in the chair whilst the work was done and the positive outcome of her lovely smile when it was all done. She told me afterwards that it all went much better than she'd imagined and it didn't even seem to last very long (even though it was over 4 hours). Her dentist couldn't believe how she relaxed she was too!

* Hold points AP20 on the forehead, touching lightly with 2 fingers of each hand whilst thinking about the stressful situation. For example, in the case of a recent argument with someone, think about what was said, how you felt at the time, where it took place, how you feel about seeing the person again

* Then after a few minutes you can change those thoughts, to feeling calmer about the situation and visualising how you would want to be when seeing the person again. You could also imagine yourself in a place where you can easily relax, by the sea, a room in your house, a walk in the country. For me it's sitting in a walled garden on a lovely summer day.

This technique can be used for many different types of stressful situations, small or large–exams, job changes, personality clashes, illness etc. It doesn't take the situation away but it does relieve the stress attached to it. You can use it for something that has already happened or something you are worried and anxious about in the future, moving house, giving a talk, starting a new job...

It brings the blood flow back to the front of the brain which helps us think rationally about the situation, rather than reacting from instinctive behaviour, as our ancestors would have done. This makes such a difference to how we perceive it.

Another quick way to relieve the effects of a stressful situation:

* Think about the stressful situation, for example in the case of a recent argument with someone, think about what was said, how you felt at the time, where it took place, how you feel about seeing the person again... and tap the points on your cheekbones directly below the middle of your eyes (AP21s)

* Then as before change those thoughts to how you would like a positive outcome

This one is very soothing:

* Rub the hollow in the middle under the ball of your foot, whilst thinking and visualising something you find calming and relaxing. It might be a sunny beach, beautiful garden or just sitting in a peaceful room at home. After a few minutes, swap to the other foot and repeat. Or even better, get someone to do this for you on both feet at the same time.

To help you move out of fear and realise your own potential and the positive outcome:

* Place your fingers on AP22
* Place your other hand on AP5 on the same side
* Hold these points together for 2–3 minutes
* Swap hands and repeat

This is very calming to do:

* Place your middle finger on the point midway between your eyebrows (third eye)
* Massage in a circular motion, taking deep, slow breaths, for a few minutes

To help with stress, teeth grinding, jaw clenching, stress headaches and neck tension:

* Hold points on the forehead, AP20s lightly, using 2 fingers of each hand whilst touching the sore spot in front of the ear where the jawbones meet, for a few minutes with the thumbs
* You can apply a little pressure with the thumbs, it will probably feel unpleasantly achy
* After a minute or so, yawn a couple of times, it should feel less sore

* Repeat 2 or 3 times
* Release the fingers and move to the sore spot in front of the jaw and massage gently

You may find yourself yawning a few times after this, which also releases tension.

There is a muscle that holds our head onto our neck, this muscle tightens when we get stressed. To release this tension:

* Feel at the back of your mouth for a soft spot, between the upper and lower jaw
* Find this spot with your finger, then push it firmly but briefly, this resets the muscle

Incidentally when done properly it is very painful!

There are points on the outside of the wrist at the base of the hand, AP17s, that really help reduce anxiety too.

When I went to Bosnia[3], we did daily visits to a home for people with disabilities. There was a lady there who was very nervous about having any sort of hands on therapy, reflexology or massage. I showed her brother how to hold these points on her hands and within a few days, she decided she would like to have a neck and shoulder massage!

* Hold the points AP17 simultaneously by putting 2 fingers onto one of the points, then use the thumb of the other hand to contact the other point
* Hold for a few minutes

Use any time when feeling anxious or a few times a day to help underlying anxiety.

Finger Holds

There can be many emotions related to stress, we can feel sad, grief, worried, fearful, guilty, angry, depressed or confused, depending on what is causing the stress and our responses to it.

FAST FIXES

When there's something on your mind and you're worried or feeling guilty about it, there can be that sinking feeling in your stomach. Holding your thumb can help release those emotions. Babies and young children will often suck their thumbs to comfort themselves.

> * Hold your thumb with your other hand for a few minutes or longer, as often as needed

Fear can make us hyperventilate and kicks in the adrenals, activating that fight or flight response. This can then make us feel more fearful. Holding the index finger helps us breathe more easily and allows that fearful feeling to dissipate. You may experience a big sigh of relief and release.

> * Hold your index finger with your other hand for a few minutes or longer, as often as needed

When people talk about the red mist that descends when we're angry, this really means that we are not seeing things clearly at all. Holding the middle finger helps us see things more clearly and see the whole picture, not just focusing on our little bit of it. It helps understanding as well as dissipating anger.

> * Hold your middle finger with your other hand for a few minutes or longer, as often as needed

To clear your head if you're feeling negative or if there is sadness and grief for a loss:

> * Hold your ring finger with your other hand for a few minutes or longer, as often as needed

If you're feeling confused about your emotions or having to push them down and pretend everything is ok, then hold the little finger. This helps us relax about the issue, so we can know our truth.

> * Hold your little finger with your other hand for a few minutes or longer, as often as needed

The fingers on the right hand are for emotions in the present and/or you are aware of what is causing it.

The fingers on the left for emotions that can be related to the past and/or you're not sure what is causing it.

Just go with which seems right at the time.

Or just do both.

> *I had a lady ring me with regard to her son who was finding school very difficult. He was getting very angry with everything in general. As you can imagine she was quite worried about him. We decided to wait a couple of weeks until the holidays before he came for an appointment. In the meantime, I talked to her about how he could hold his middle finger when he was feeling angry and she could hold her thumb for feeling worried about him. When they came for his appointment a couple of weeks later, she was amazed how much he had calmed down already and how much more positive she felt herself! Definitely a good result and such a simple thing to do.*

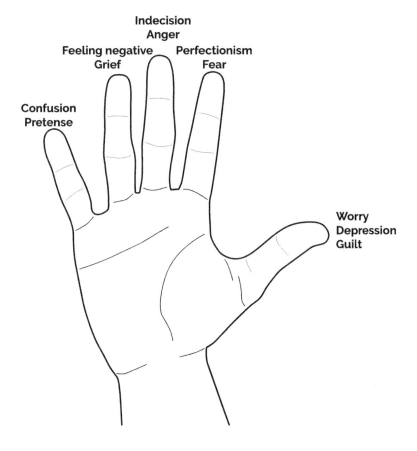

Bach Flower Remedies

A very gentle and very effective way to diffuse stressful emotions is using Bach Flower Remedies, you've probably already heard of Rescue Remedy which is a combination of 5 remedies to help with shock, emergencies or accidents.

There are 38 different remedies relating to different emotional states, a few drops in a glass of water sipped throughout the day diffuses those emotional states.

A fantastic example of this is clearly demonstrated by how these remedies helped my daughter's rabbits. Originally house rabbits, they were very happy to be handled and stroked, but like all rabbits, they didn't like being picked up. And of course, as house rabbits there was no need for them to be picked up.

When my daughter and rabbits moved in with us temporarily, they became outdoor rabbits, in a hutch overnight and then being carried to and from a run in the garden during the day.

Bob didn't seem to mind too much after a few initial struggles but Dave (the female) struggled and became very anxious about the whole thing. Her heart would race, she would really struggle to get free, she cried and then she started pulling her fur out after each time she was moved, it was heart breaking to see. I remembered the Bach Flowers, so we checked the list and chose Rock Rose for terror, panic and a sense of helplessness, all of which fitted this situation.

We put a couple of drops in their water and Dave immediately stopped the fur pulling and crying. A few weeks later she started again, it turned out my daughter had stopped putting the drops in the water as Dave seemed fine! We started with the drops again and all was well after that. You can see how effective these truly are.

Because emotional states can lead to physical ailments, keeping ourselves emotionally healthy can be a great preventative of physical ill health. Using the Bach Flowers remedies is a great way to address and dissolve negative emotional states.

There are plenty of books about the remedies that you can explore for more information, however here is a quick reference guide[4]

Agrimony—mental torture behind a cheerful face

Aspen—fear of unknown things

Beech—intolerance

Centaury—the inability to say 'no'

Cerato—lack of trust in one's own decisions

Cherry Plum—fear of the mind giving way

Chestnut Bud—failure to learn from mistakes

Chicory—selfish, possessive love

Clematis—dreaming of the future without working in the present

Crab Apple—the cleansing remedy, also for not liking something about ourselves

Elm—overwhelmed by responsibility

Gentian—discouragement after a setback

Gorse—hopelessness and despair

Heather—talkative self-concern and being self-centred

Holly—hatred, envy and jealousy

Honeysuckle—living in the past

Hornbeam—tiredness at the thought of doing something

Impatiens—impatience

Larch—lack of confidence

Mimulus—fear of known things

Mustard—deep gloom for no reason

Oak—the plodder who keeps going past the point of exhaustion

Olive—exhaustion following mental or physical effort

Pine—guilt

Red Chestnut—over-concern for the welfare of loved ones

Rock Rose—terror and fright

Rock Water—self-denial, rigidity and self-repression

Scleranthus—inability to choose between alternatives

Star of Bethlehem—shock

Sweet Chestnut—extreme mental anguish, when everything has been tried and there is no light left

Vervain—over-enthusiasm

Vine—dominance and inflexibility

Walnut—protection from change and unwanted influences

Water Violet—quiet self-reliance leading to isolation

White Chestnut—unwanted thoughts and mental arguments

Wild Oat—uncertainty over one's direction in life

Wild Rose—drifting, resignation, apathy

Willow—self-pity and resentment

Rescue Remedy is a combination of Star of Bethlehem, Rock Rose, Clematis, Impatiens and Cherry Plum, for stressful situations, shock and emergencies.

The Vagus Nerve

Until recently it was not known or understood how much the vagus nerve has an impact on the state of our health. The vagus nerve is connected to most of the organs in the body and has a two-way communication with virtually all of those organs and the brain.

Normally the vagus nerve helps the efficient function of the organs in the body. In partnership with the parasympathetic nervous system, it is associated with rest, relaxation, digestion and regeneration.

You may be familiar with the fight or flight response of the sympathetic nervous system to stressful situations and danger. There is also a third response to extreme threat which is a survival response leading to "freeze" mode.

This disconnects us from what is going on, leaving us feeling frozen, numb or "not here". The vagus nerve plays its part to protect us from harm and conserving energy.

Ideally, we should spend life in a relaxed and calm state, responding to stressful situations and then after they have passed, reverting back to the relaxed state again. Unfortunately, we spend much of our time these days in a relatively stressed state due to the worries and pressures of everyday life (see section on 'Stress') which activates the sympathetic nervous system. This can lead to chronic disease. When the freeze mode is activated for sustained periods this can lead to a feeling of being in shutdown mode, which is often experienced by people with chronic fatigue.

Research by neurosurgeon Kevin Tracy has shown that the vagus nerve also influences inflammation[5].

When the vagus nerve is toned, the inflammatory action is switched off. As inflammation is implicated in much disease in the body, then we can see just how important the vagus nerve is for our health.

Constant activation of the fight or flight response (sympathetic nervous system) can switch off the organs of our immune system, the spleen, the thymus and the gut (there are immune cells in the gut lining too), so you can see how much damage constant stress can do to our bodies.

The body can start to heal when the vagus nerve is toned or "happy", which is only when the parasympathetic nervous system is turned on and the sympathetic nervous system is off. This relaxation response will slow down breathing and heart rate, stimulate digestion and allow relaxation and feeling calm.

Studies[6] have shown that anxiety and learned fear in rats is regulated by the gut. Because the vagus nerve connects the gut to the brain emotionally, so our "gut feeling" is very real!

As it is connected to the brain, a toned vagus nerve will also help calm our moods and reduce anxiety and depression.

When the vagus nerve is lacking in tone, then we can see these symptoms:

- Inability to relax
- insomnia
- obesity and weight gain
- diabetes
- brain fog
- IBS
- anxiety
- depression
- chronic fatigue
- high or low heart rate
- heartburn
- dizziness/fainting
- B12 deficiency
- chronic inflammation
- allergies
- heart palpitations
- migraines
- fibromyalgia
- tinnitus
- memory disorders
- mood disorders
- leaky gut
- autoimmune disorders

For more information on the vagus nerve and gut health: The Polyvagal Theory by Dr Stephen Porges.

FAST FIXES

This helps all the cranial nerves, especially the vagus nerve, which contribute to calming the body's autonomic nervous system, releasing anxiety. Use this often.

* Interlink the fingers of both hands and put your hands behind your head, covering the base of the skull and the hollows beneath this

* Then keeping your head still, move your eyes to the right, until you take a deep breath or feel a sigh coming on

* Bring your eyes back to the centre

* Repeat the eye movement to the other side

If you don't notice a sigh or a deep breath, just keep the eyes in position for about a minute, each side, use as often as you like.

Another way to help calm anxiety and the effects of stress is to:

* Hold one hand on top of the head
* Place the fingertips of the other hand on the point midway between the breasts. This point is aptly named "The Sea of Tranquillity" hold together for a few minutes

This is also part of the Main Central Vertical Acupressure flow which has a number of benefits (see section on 'Preventative Health').

A good combination for calming anxiety whilst helping energy levels too:

* Place the fingertips of one hand on the point midway between the breasts, on the acupressure point "The Sea of Tranquillity"
* Place the other hand just below the navel, this point is "The Sea of Vitality" hold together for a few minutes

This is also very calming to do:

* Place your middle finger on the point midway between your eyebrows (third eye)
* Massage in a circular motion, taking deep, slow breaths, for a few minutes

If fear and anxiety are holding you back from doing something that will have a positive impact on your physical, mental and emotional health:

* Hold the point AP22 just below the collarbone, next to the sternum, with one hand
* With the other hand touch AP5 on the inside of the ankle

* Hold together for 2–3 minutes
* Then move both hands to the points on the other side of the body
* Hold for 2–3 minutes

Another combination that can help you move forward physically, mentally and emotionally are:

* Hold the point on the inside of the knee, AP1 with one hand
* With the other hand touch AP5 on the inside of the ankle
* Hold together for 2–3 minutes
* Then move both hands to the points on the other leg
* Hold for 2–3 minutes

This is such a simple thing to do and I've seen many benefits for clients from using this. Things like how they view difficult situations, reducing the fear and anxiety in regard to a new job, relationship break ups, moving house and more. It certainly helped me during an incredibly stressful time and saw me through it to the other side.

This is very calming but also helps re-energise you, as it hooks up all the meridians to allow the energy to flow:

* Cross one ankle over the other
* Then cross the same side arm over the other arm
* Link your fingers together
* Then bring hands up together so that they rest against your chest
* Bring your tongue up to the roof of your mouth
* Hold this position for 2–3 minutes

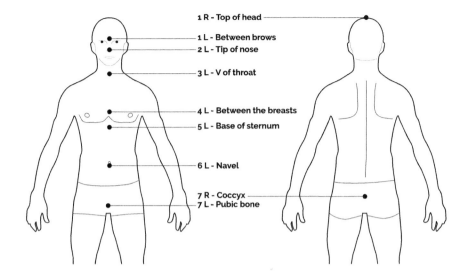

The labels on the figure read:

1 R - Top of head
1 L - Between brows
2 L - Tip of nose
3 L - V of throat
4 L - Between the breasts
5 L - Base of sternum
6 L - Navel
7 R - Coccyx
7 L - Pubic bone

The Main Central Vertical Energy Flow will also calm the vagus nerve. It is great for helping the back, the nervous system, the digestive system, the chakras and the meridian energies. I like to think it re aligns our whole system.

For more information on how this can help you, please see section on 'Preventative Health'.

* Place your right hand on the top of your head, this remains there until the last step
* Place your left middle finger on the third eye (between the eyebrows) for 2–3 minutes
* Move your left middle finger to the tip of nose, hold for 2–3 minutes
* Move your left middle finger to the "V" of the throat, hold for 2–3 minutes
* Move your left middle finger to the sternum, between the breasts, hold for 2–3 minutes
* Move your left middle finger to the base of sternum (solar plexus) hold for 2–3 minutes

* Move your left middle finger to the navel, hold for 2–3 minutes
* Move your left middle finger to the centre of the pubic bone, hold for 2–3 minutes
* Move your right hand (palm side or back) onto the coccyx, keeping your left hand on the pubic bone. Hold these points for 2–3 minutes

It will probably take you 15–20 minutes, but you can do this whilst reading or watching TV if you like.

Other ways to stimulate the vagus nerve and reduce stress and inflammation, that you can easily introduce into your lifestyle:

* Slowly stroking down from the back of ears along the neck to the collarbones 4 or 5 times, soothes the vagus nerve
* Deep slow breathing and also making the outbreath longer
* A cold shower or even just splashing your face with cold water
* Singing, chanting or humming
* Playing a musical instrument, especially a wind instrument
* Yawning helps reset the brain as well as the vagus nerve
* Yoga
* Laughter and smiling
* Social interaction
* Prayer and meditation
* Probiotics and a wholefood diet
* Mild exercise
* Gargling
* Gratitude and kindness

All of these soothe the vagus nerve, it just comes down to personal choice and some are easier to add in to your day than others.

There will probably be more of an impact from doing these exercises little and often, rather than once every now and again for a longer period. Although you can of course do both.

Dips in energy during the day

These can be from lack of sleep, early starts, overwork, too much to do, worrying, low blood sugar levels or too much carbohydrate.

A carbohydrate lunch (sandwich/bagel/pasta salad) can often make us feel sleepy anyway. In Chinese medicine, 1–3pm is when the small intestine energy is at its height, for good reason, in a lot of countries this is the time for the main meal of the day. As the digestive system can use up to 70% of the body's energy, you can see why there is that mid-afternoon slump.

One easy way to avoid this, is to eat more protein and less carbohydrate for lunch, so for instance choosing a tuna salad rather than a cheese sandwich, this will have less of a sopoforic effect on the body, allowing us to stay more alert.

6–8 glasses of water a day will help re-energise you and help flush out toxins.

The body depends on water for good performance, clear thinking and body and mind function. Without pure water the body's electrical system is impaired and the lymphatic system and organ function suffers. Dehydration can bring about sudden fatigue and temporary confusion.

Research shows that people who drank 5 or more glasses of water were significantly less likely to suffer from a heart attack[7], kidney or bladder problems, dry skin, constipation and some types of back problems[8].

FAST FIXES

For a quick energy boost at any time of day try this Meridian Flush:

* Using the hands, run them lightly just off the body from the big toes up the front of the legs and torso to the armpits
* Run each hand in turn from the armpit along the inside of the arm to the finger ends along the palm of the hand
* Turn the hand over and run up from the finger tips along back of the hand, arm, shoulder, to the ear
* Repeat along the other arm
* Then using both hands, go from the ears to the forehead, then along the top of the head down the back all the way to the feet
* Repeat this sequence 2 more times

When teaching a workshop on High Touch Acupressure, I was demonstrating this on one lady and she leapt forward as I brushed in the energy field over the area across the back of her neck. I hadn't actually touched her, but she had definitely felt it! It turned out she had a longstanding neck problem which was quite painful in that area. Running the meridians had obviously cleared some sort of energy blockage there. When I saw her a couple of weeks later, she told me the pain had totally gone, which she was very happy about.

Another way of working the meridian energies is by gently but firmly massaging the ears—all over the whole ear, inside and out, front and back. This stimulates all the acupuncture points on the ears (there is a whole mini acupuncture system on the ear). Not only does it stimulate the acupuncture points and hence the energy flow in the body, it also helps the blood flow to the brain, helping get rid of "brain fog" and also neck pain. Try it if your neck feels painful or sore when turning the head, you will notice the difference immediately.

* Firmly massage both ears—all over the whole ear, inside and out, front and back

This can help clear daily fatigue:

* Put the fingers of your left hand onto AP19 in the right elbow
* Bend your right arm and place your hand over your right shoulder on AP3
* Hold together for 2–3 minutes
* Repeat on opposite side

Use as often as you like daily.

Cross-crawl is basically marching or walking on the spot moving one arm and opposite leg at the same time in co-ordination, then doing the same with the other arm and opposite leg. Cross-crawl activates many different muscles in the body, stimulating the connection between the right and left halves of the brain by forming more neural networks, so it is also a very powerful exercise to stimulate and improve brain function.

Marching on the spot improves your concentration, co-ordination, memory and lymph flow. Cross-crawl movements also activate the speech and language centres of the brain.

It encourages the natural rhythm of the **cerebrospinal fluid**, which acts as a shock absorber, protecting the brain tissue, spinal cord and all nerves enervating from the spine, from injury. Every time we breathe and the ribcage moves, the cerebrospinal fluid is pumped from the brain down the spine and back to the brain, nourishing the nerves and organs in the body.

It is also a good exercise to do to feel more energised:

* Make exaggerated movements as per the diagram
* Move opposite arm to opposite leg, then swap
* Repeat about 30 times

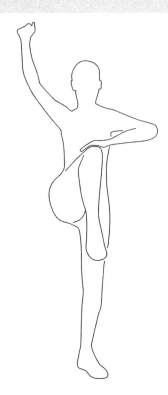

Here is a quick routine to help wake up the body, tapping these points will help the body function more effectively.

This brings calm before the day ahead:

* First, using the tips of your fingers, tap the points on the cheekbone just below the eyes St1

This helps to increase our energy:

> * Then tap the points shown just underneath the
>   collarbone K27

This helps the thymus, great for the immune system, remember Tarzan used to thump his chest to gather his strength!

> * Tap the point on the breastbone

These are great to help get your mind on track for planning and organising your day.

> * Lastly tap the points shown on the ribcage Sp NLs

Tap each set about 30 times fairly quickly and use as often as you like daily.

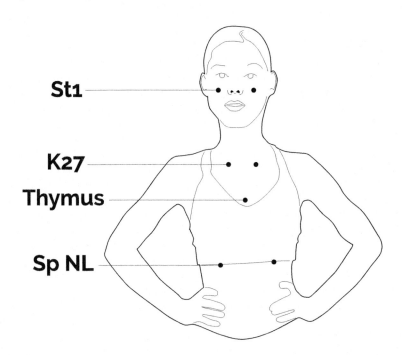

St1

K27

Thymus

Sp NL

If you're feeling a bit spaced out, a bit faint or disorientated, this is a really quick way to feel more "with it".

* Put 2 fingers of one hand onto the space between your nose and top lip
* Put your thumb onto the space between your lower lip and chin
* Press and rub both of these points firmly for about 15 seconds
* Repeat if necessary

I had a client who was in her late teens and suffering from ME. She recovered very well from her sessions, but the one thing she was left with was being prone to fainting every now and again. We found that using these points herself if she felt it coming on, really helped to stop it happening.

She also showed her friends what to do, if it happened while she was with them. They were so well versed in it that when they had a first aid demonstration at school, at the end when the volunteer was placed in the recovery position, one friend told the instructor "Don't forget to press her points!"

Pain

Black's Medical Dictionary 37th Edition 1992 states:

> 'The ability to perceive pain constitutes a special sense which the body has evolved, in order that it may preserve itself by avoiding conditions that produce damage.'

Pain is a localised sensation ranging from mild discomfort to an excruciating experience. Signals are referred back through the central nervous system (CNS) to the brain from the area where there is trauma or injury.

Pain is the result of stimulation of special sensory nerve endings, there are 2 types of pain receptors:

Mechanoreceptors are part of the muscle proprioceptive system which feeds back information about the position and tightness of muscles. These are involved in fibromyalgia, muscle aches as well as pain from injury to muscles.

Nociceptors are free nerve endings found in most tissue in the body (exception brain and intestines). Pain can originate in skin, muscles, joints or visceral tissue (organs). Things like distension, dilation, slight ischaemia, irritant chemical substances, prolonged muscular contraction or spasm can all stimulate these nociceptors excessively.

Referred pain is felt in an area other than the one with the injury or disease. Some sensory nerves converge together before entering the brain so the brain is confused as to where the signals originate.

Pain management

There is no pain until the message gets to the brain, the stimulus goes through the central nervous system, then via the thalamus into the cerebral cortex, which then manifests pain in the area of the stimulus.

Pain is made worse by lack of sleep, disturbed sleep leads to reduced serotonin levels which leads to lowered pain thresholds. It also leads to a biochemical imbalance reducing levels of growth hormone which is needed for repair of muscle and tissue damage.

By using methods to reduce pain, sleep patterns are better, hence there is less pain and more repair of damage.

Some techniques are based on changing the brains interpretation of signals by interrupting the pain impulse.

Touch messages get to the brain faster than pain messages. You will already know that if you bang your knee your first impulse is to rub it. Rubbing or massaging helps physiologically, by bringing warmth and increasing the blood flow to the area. It also changes the proprioceptor messages which then alter the tension in the muscle. Massage also helps neurologically, by diminishing the pain messages.

Somatic stimulation inhibits transmission of pain signals, this can be pressure on the area, cold, heat, vibration or counter irritant substances, all of these are of course dependant on the nature of the injury or trauma.

All of the above compete with the pain signals in the spinal cord (Gate Control Theory) and activate the production of endorphins, which are the body's own natural painkillers. This in effect closes the gate to pain signals. Anxiety, excitement will keep the gate open. So, you can see that when we are tense, anxious or upset, this can make the pain feel worse.

Therapies such as massage, kinesiology, reflexology, acupuncture, acupressure, and other therapies using touch will all encourage the release of endorphins.

Factors contributing to pain signals can be mechanical, for example poor posture, injury or trauma that causes postural imbalances. Food or chemical intolerances, or nutritional deficiencies can also be a causal factor. A build-up of toxins due to poor elimination can contribute. Emotional stressors and perception of pain, often based on past experience can have an effect on pain too.

Many of these pain relief techniques are based on energy therapies—removing obstructions to the free flow of energy, not only reducing pain but also helping to eliminate the problems associated with it.

Pain relief and Injury recall

A memory of every past injury is stored in the body (held in joints and ligaments), and can be detrimental to the person in terms of residual pain, loss of flexibility and mobility, both physically and mentally.

Injury recall removes injury memory from the body, reducing pain and making the body less susceptible to future injury and energy depletion. You can use this technique on any type of past or present physical injury, including sprains, falls, anaesthetic, toothache, scar tissue, the jaw, operations etc.

When using it for toothache, touch the tooth at the gum line. Using this pain technique may not make it go away entirely, depending on the problem, but it should help reduce the effects of trauma to the area.

FAST FIX

This technique is different from most of the others in that you only need to do it once per injury. It is probably easier to ask someone else to do this for you.

* Put your hand over the injury site
* The other person holds your heel still with one hand and then grasps the top of your foot on the same side as the injury (if relevant) and tugs it firmly down towards the sole of the foot, 3 or 4 times

* Repeat with the other foot

This actually not only helps further healing of the trauma; it has been demonstrated to increase the flexibility of the joints and allow further movement of the hips and shoulders.

Emotional Stress Release (ESR) for pain

At the time of the physical injury or trauma there is always an emotional component involved.

This is an excellent technique to use when you can after a physical injury and also if long standing pain is draining you emotionally.

There are points on the forehead that help release the emotional stress attached to a situation and balance hormone levels in relation to that situation. These points are excellent for any stress, not just pain.

FAST FIXES

* Place one hand on the painful area
* Using your thumb and two fingers of the other hand, lightly touch the points on the forehead, AP20s
* Think about where the pain is located
* Think about the quality of the pain, what it feels like when it hurts, whether it is a sharp pain or achy, sore, if it's there all of the time or just some of the time and when it occurs
* Think about what actually happened to cause the pain, where you were and what you were doing when it happened, i.e. the memory associated with the pain
* Then after a few minutes you can change those thoughts, feeling calmer and visualising how you would feel and be without the pain

I've found so many times with clients that just using these two techniques (Injury Recall and ESR) at the beginning of a session has drastically decreased the person's pain level. They also help the body's healing process.

Pain usually has some sort of stress associated with it, this technique helps with that and it is amazing how much it can reduce and often remove the pain.

> * Touch the painful area and tap AP21 on each side, about 30 times, to reduce stress and in turn reduce the pain

You can also use this point when getting stressed, for instance when you're running late and stuck in a traffic jam, think about that stress and tap both AP21s.

Pain in general

This very simple technique can help with pain in general in the body.

> * Hold the points AP16 and AP5 together on the affected side for a few minutes
> * You can also hold the points on the opposite side as well if you wish
> * Repeat as often as you like

In reflexology there is a technique called Cross Reflexes. When an area is painful and sore, rather than massage that area directly which may not be beneficial, you can massage the corresponding cross reflex. So, for painful toes, you can massage the corresponding fingers. If the big toe and second toe on the left foot are sore then you would massage the thumb and index finger on the left hand for example.

Here are the cross reflexes:

> * For toes—massage the corresponding fingers

* For fingers—massage the corresponding toes
* For wrists—massage the corresponding ankle
* For ankles—massage the corresponding wrist
* For elbows—massage the corresponding knee
* For knees—massage the corresponding elbow

Muscle pain

This works well for muscle aches and pains that don't seem resolve themselves as quickly as you would expect and when other muscles start to get affected too.

FAST FIX

Move the affected area around, gently, so you can feel the tight and painful areas before you start.

* Touch the points AP20s with your thumb and 2 fingers of the other hand
* Place the thumb and finger tips of one hand around your navel
* Whilst keeping the hand on the forehead still, push in with the fingers of the other hand and stimulate with a circular motion for about 30 seconds
* Now put your thumb pads onto the nail of your index fingers
* Keeping your thumbs in this position, touch the points AP20s on the forehead with middle and ring fingers of both hands for about a minute
* Visualise those muscles that feel tight, relaxing and feeling much easier, for about a minute

Again, move the affected area around, gently, so you can feel the improvement.

You can repeat this as often as you like.

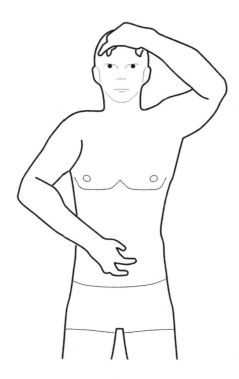

Pain relief and temporal tap

In temporal tap we tap over the temporal bone around the upper part and back of the ears, here there is a big concentration of nerves, where all sensory inputs are filtered.

The nervous system is usually bombarded by many stimuli and some of them are unnecessary. Temporal tap filters or brings to our awareness what is relevant to us at that time so the brain can listen to it and act upon it.

When there is pain it is possible that the brain is not fully processing the pain messages, so temporal tap brings back the brain's awareness to these messages which then increases the neural and chemical activity to enable the body to deal with it.

This technique is also very effective for post operational pain and scar tissue.

FAST FIX

* To use this on yourself, touch the painful area with your right hand
* Tap firmly on the skull around the back of the left ear with your left hand, from the top to the bottom 5 or 6 times

Pain relief and cross-crawl

Cross-crawl is basically marching or walking on the spot moving one arm and opposite leg at the same time in co-ordination, then doing the same with the other arm and opposite leg. Cross-crawl activates many different muscles in the body improving the connection between the right and left halves of the brain by forming more neural networks, so it is also a very powerful exercise to stimulate and enhance brain function.

Marching on the spot improves your concentration, co-ordination, memory and lymph flow. Cross-crawl movements also activate the speech and language centres of the brain.

It encourages the natural rhythm of the **cerebrospinal fluid**, which acts as a shock absorber, protecting the brain tissue, spinal cord and all nerves enervating from the spine, from injury. Every time we breathe and the ribcage moves, the cerebrospinal fluid is pumped from the brain down the spine and back to the brain, nourishing the nerves and organs in the body.

By touching the painful area and cross-crawling we are helping the Cerebrospinal Fluid and hence the Central Nervous System to do something about the pain messages going from the pain site to the brain.

FAST FIX

* Make exaggerated movements as per the diagram
* Move opposite arm to opposite leg a few times, then swap

* Then touch the affected area and cross-crawl again at the same time 20–30 times

You may have to improvise how you do this depending on where the painful area is.

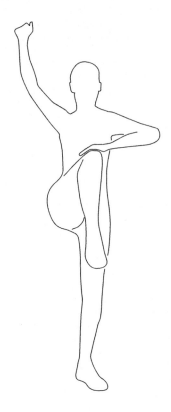

Head points for pain in specific areas of the body

These points have a relationship with various neurotransmitters in the body. Tapping these points stimulates the release of the relevant neurotransmitter, which has an action on the painful area. These head points relate to different areas of the body which are shown on the meridian chart. The meridian chart shows the numbers to use for the head points.

Use the chart to find out which meridian pathway is closest to where the pain is. If for instance your elbow is sore, check whether it is the back of the elbow (area 5) or the inside (area 5), or it may be more to the thumb side (area 1) or little finger side (area 6).

If it is somewhere along the spinal area of the back, the you would use point number 7, whereas if it was on the back away from the spinal area, then you would choose point number 3.

The back of the leg would correspond to 3, the front would be 2, the outside would be 4 and the inside could be 3 or 4, depending on which meridian it is closest to.

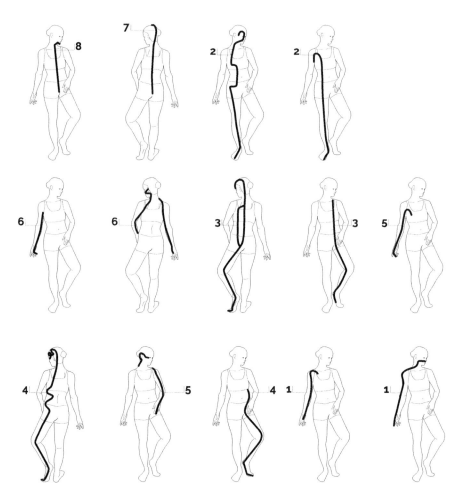

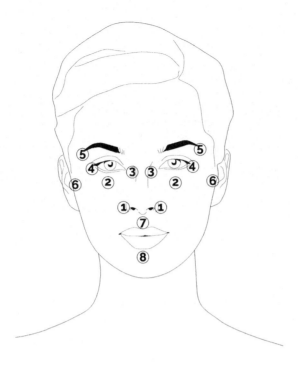

FAST FIXES

In all cases tap the point very quickly about 100 times and on the same side as the pain.

For pain of duration 1 week –1 month:

* Tap the point related to painful area on same side of body

For pain from an older injury (over 1 month):

* Touch the painful area with one hand and use the other to tap the relevant point. It can be helpful if you move the area as point is tapped, this may not be possible at first but as you tap the range of movement will increase as the pain decreases

There are amino acids that nutritionally support these head points, if the pain responds to these points but comes back, it may be worth supplementing with the appropriate amino acid for a while.

HEAD POINT	ACUPUNCTURE POINT	AMINO ACID
1	LI 20	Glycine
2	St 1	Histamine
3	B 1	Tryptophan
4	GB 1	Choline
5	TW 23	Inositol
6	SI 19	Tyrosine

Pain at the same time every day

Pain is telling us that there is a problem in that area, so if you have a pain that is new or something like a sprain or a broken ankle, then obviously you wouldn't want to remove the pain and start walking on it again as this would cause further damage.

But for chronic or longstanding pain this technique is great. It may not help what has caused the pain, but by removing the pain it can help take some of the stress off the body. This can then give your body the chance to rest and heal.

Energy circulates around the body in the meridian pathways and each meridian has a time when the energy flow is at its peak. Pain is often associated with over energy in a meridian. If pain occurs around the same time each day or gets worse, then there may be over energy in the meridian that is most active at that particular time, e.g. back pain which is worse in the evening, then this could be related to too much energy in the Kidney meridian (time 5–7pm). Sedating this can reduce the over energy, restoring balance. These acupuncture points will sedate the over energy in the meridian, so any pain associated with this time of day will reduce.

This can be beneficial if you have pain at night, in the knee, shoulder, back or neck for instance.

FAST FIXES

Here are the meridian times and relevant tapping points:

MERIDIAN	ABBREVIATION	TIME	TAPPING POINT
Stomach	St	7–9am	St 41
Spleen	Sp	9–11am	Sp 2
Heart	H	11–1pm	H 9
Small Intestine	SI	1–3pm	SI 3
Bladder	B	3–5pm	B 67
Kidney	K	5–7pm	K 7
Circulation Sex	CX	7–9pm	CX 9
Triple Warmer	TW	9–11pm	TW 3
Gall Bladder	GB	11–1am	GB 43
Liver	Lv	1–3am	Lv 8
Lung	L	3–5am	L 9
Large intestine	LI	5–7am	LI 11

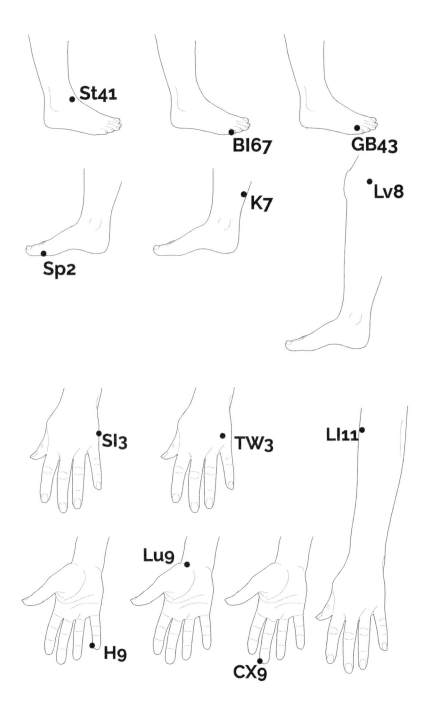

* Look up time of day on chart and its relevant tapping point
* Tap the point on the opposite side of the body as the pain
* About 30 taps at a beat of 1 tap per second
* Reassess the pain and if it is still there, tap on the same side of the body as the pain, again 30 taps
* Reassess the pain and if it is still there, tap on the opposite side of the body as the pain, again 30 taps
* Stop when either the pain has gone or it is reduced and further tapping doesn't seem to change it anymore

This can be done at any time of day not just the time it occurs.

This really helped one of my clients for her back pain, which was always really intense for the first 2 hours when she got up. This related to 7–9am, which is the Stomach meridian. Tapping St 41 immediately took the pain right down from a 9 (out of 10) to a 3. Further work took it right down to a zero.

Scars

Often a wound will heal well but leave a scar that can still be uncomfortable or painful.

FAST FIX

* Place the north side of a magnet on the painful area and leave for anything up to 20 minutes, repeat as often as necessary

I had a young client who had a scar from a recent operation that was very uncomfortable. I used the magnet with her and she was amazed to realise the discomfort had gone by the end of the session.

Chronic pain and food

Acute pain hurts when you move the area and then gets worse the more you move it, whereas chronic pain hurts when the area is first moved, then eases off somewhat.

Chronic pain can be related to intolerances so it's worth consulting a kinesiologist to find out what they are and remove them from your diet temporarily.

The most common food intolerances are: wheat, milk, eggs, corn, soya and members of the nightshade family which are potatoes, tomatoes, peppers, aubergines.

People suffering from chronic pain often have lower levels of endorphins; DLPA (DL–Phenylalanine) helps to restore normal levels. It can help alleviate long-term chronic pain but doesn't interfere with body's natural defence mechanisms for short-term acute pain. Do not take if pregnant or if you have phenylketonuria, heart problems or high blood pressure.

Foods with pain killing activity include chilli peppers, cloves, garlic, ginger, liquorice, onion, peppermint, blueberries, cherries, dried currants, curry powder, dried dates, gherkins, paprika, prunes, raspberries and to a lesser extent, almonds, Granny Smith apples, oranges, persimmons (Sharron Fruit), pineapples, tea and peppers.

Vitamin C is excellent for wound healing as well as for reducing inflammation and helping with stress.

Menstrual pain

FAST FIX

You can use these pain tapping points for menstrual pain:

* Tap the points Sp 2 (see page 56)
* About 30 taps at a beat of 1 tap per second

* Reassess pain and if it is still there, tap again, 30 taps
* Stop when either the pain has gone or it is reduced and further tapping doesn't seem to change it anymore

I shared this with a client who was having very painful periods. She told me that when the pains started and she did the tapping, at first nothing happened, then 3 minutes later the pain stopped. She continued to do it for the next few days and she said that although she could tell there was still some cramping, the pain just wasn't there anymore.

Cramps

These can affect all of us at some point in our lives and it can be down to an imbalance of minerals in the body.

Quinine which is in tonic water is a well-known remedy and easy to implement, however it's not an immediate quick fix.

It is often the leg muscles, the calf in particular that cramp up. The spindle cell mechanism gets out of kilter and sends messages to the muscle fibres to contract and overtighten. If we can reset those cells, then this will then relieve the cramping muscle.

Have you ever been sat in a chair and started to nod off, your head droops further and further down, until suddenly your head shoots back upright with a jolt? The body has realised your neck muscles are not doing their job and so it immediately resets the spindle cells in the neck, so that those muscles are supporting the head again.

The spindle cells are at the centre of the muscle fibres and a feathering touch will confuse them and allow them to reset themselves, which relieves the cramp.

FAST FIX

* Use your fingertips to very lightly and rapidly "patter" the centre of the affected muscle

You can usually gauge where you would do this, as it is where the pain is.

As a guide, for cramps in the calf or the foot this would be halfway between knee and ankle at the back of the leg. In the quads at the front of the thigh, halfway between knee and groin. For the triceps at the back of the arm, halfway between elbow and shoulder.

If you get a lot of muscle cramps, try doing this regularly to reduce the frequency:

* With tips of your fingers hold the AP8s at the outer back of the knees for a few minutes

Repetitive Strain Injury

Any joint, muscle or tendon can be subject to Repetitive Strain Injury if overused over a period of time. Muscles will tend to "switch off" if there is injury or trauma, this increases the risk of injury to the surrounding tissues. There are simple techniques to switch these muscles back on, which then relieves the stress on the surrounding tissue.

Possibly one of the most common repetitive strains these days are the wrists, due to working with computers and laptops. Occupational health can help and prevent in the long term.

Immediate relief can be gained from massaging the base of the thumb and little finger along with the areas where the hands join the wrist at each side of the hand.

FAST FIXES

Work on the hand that is affected, if it's both then do both.

* Use the thumb or fingers of the other hand to massage along the 2nd joint of the thumb on the palm side
* Using the thumb or fingers again to massage along the joint at the very base of the thumb on the palm side where it joins the wrist

* Use the thumb or fingers of the other hand to massage along the 3rd joint of the little finger on the palm side
* Using the thumb or fingers again, massage along the joint at the base of the palm on the little finger side where it joins the wrist

I gave a talk on food intolerances for a group of ladies who were wanting to lose weight. One of the ladies asked me afterwards about her arthritic hands and thumbs. I showed her how this technique could help her, she couldn't believe the immediate pain relief. I saw her the following week and she had been doing this most days and her hands were still pain free.

If there is tenderness, soreness and stiffness in just the thumb, then you only need to do the first 2 steps on the affected thumb.

Worth doing daily for both wrists and thumbs.

This helps with wrist pain:

* Cross your arms, and place your fingers in the creases of the elbows on the thumb side
* Hold for 2–3 minutes

Insomnia

Deep sleep is essential for health, we can have the odd disturbed night without too much impact on the body, but in the long-term poor sleep can cause big problems.

Research[9] has shown that less sleep can make you 4–6 times more likely to catch a cold, so sleep is vital for the immune system.

Poor sleep and the resulting tiredness can affect the brain, contributing to brain fog, lack of concentration and poor memory. (See section on 'Brain fog, etc')

Sleep deprivation can affect our hunger hormones and increase stress hormones, which then make us crave unhealthy foods. This can impact on insulin activity and could eventually lead to type 2 diabetes.

Eating more fibre rich foods throughout the day helps us reduce those night time sugar/carb cravings, by feeding the good bacteria in the gut. These bacteria produce chemicals that reduce stress and anxiety and also help immunity.

FAST FIXES

* Take a good probiotic daily and make sure there are plenty of good fibre foods in your diet

When you can't get off to sleep or you wake during the night and your mind is racing and full of thoughts, this technique is great for stilling the mind.

* Hold both AP4s for a few minutes

This is quite easy to do while lying in bed before going to sleep, or if you wake during the night.

Use this technique if you are upset, stressed or anxious about something specific. It can be done before going to bed or, if you wake up during the night you can use it then too.

* Hold the AP20 points on the forehead lightly, using 2 fingers of each hand while thinking about not being able to get to sleep, or waking during the night–and how you feel about it

* If you are aware of something specific that is stopping you from sleeping, you can think about that as well

* Then after a few minutes you can change those thoughts–visualise sleeping through the night, waking up refreshed and how you would feel in the morning after a good night's sleep

Use this to improve sleep patterns and sleep quality:

* Spread the fingers of one hand along the bottom of front ribcage

* Then tap the point shown in the hollow just in front of the midline of the ear, on one side of the face

* Repeat on the other side

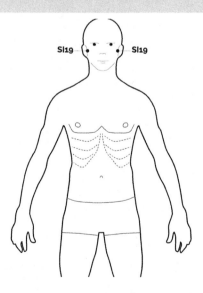

Stimulating this point helps with sleep too, use it just before going to bed.

* Rub the point AP17 in the crease of the wrist directly below the little finger on the palm side of the hand
* Repeat on other hand if you wish

Headaches

Headaches can be very debilitating, stopping us from enjoying life and performing our daily tasks. The brain needs fuel for energy, water and oxygen to function efficiently. If any of these are lacking, then the body tries to increase the amount by dilating the blood vessels to the brain. This can then put pressure on the pain receptors in these vessels, triggering pain and the end result is a headache!

There are also other factors which can contribute to having a headache.

FAST FIXES

Water helps dilute toxins so the kidneys can process them. There needs to be sufficient water in the body to allow this to happen. If there isn't then the kidneys will take it from elsewhere in the body, including the brain. When the brain is dehydrated, it can actually shrink in size which can trigger the pain receptors, resulting in a headache.

Caffeine can also dehydrate the body, as the kidneys have to work harder to remove it.

* Drink a couple of glasses of water, then keep hydrated by drinking water throughout the day

Make drinking water a regular habit.

For headaches in general:

* Hold AP7 with same side AP12 for a few minutes
* Swap hands and repeat

For headaches in general, sinus headaches and also stress headaches:

Hold these acupressure points for a few minutes on each set of points:

* Both AP20s together
* Both AP21s together
* Both AP22s together

These points are also good for clearing the sinuses.

For a headache that feels "toxic":

* Hold the part of the head where the pain is with one hand and with the other contact AP11 (on whichever side is more comfortable), hold together for a few minutes

Facial reflex and acupressure points that will help:

* Using the middle fingers press gently, starting at the inner corner of the eyebrows and moving slowly along the bony parts of the eye sockets around the eye, until you reach the start point
* Press the points at the inner corner of the eyebrows for 5—10 seconds
* Press the points next to the nose, halfway down the nose for 5—10 seconds
* Press the points next to the nose, at the bottom of the nose for 5—10 seconds
* Do all of this sequence three times

This sequence is also good to help release sinus congestion.

I have used these points with many clients. Once they knew which point worked best, they could then use that one for self-help if they needed to.

1st GB 20 at the base of the skull

2nd SI 18 about an inch in front of the midpoint of the ear, there is a hollow here

3rd B 2 the inner edge of the eyebrow

4th St 1 on the cheekbone directly below the eye

5th LI 2 at the base of the index finger (thumb side)

6th SI 5 in the hollow at the junction of palm and wrist (little finger side)

* Hold the above acupressure points bilaterally and simultaneously in the given order
* Press quite firmly on each point, breathe out through your mouth and relax
* Be aware which point is giving you most relief, go back to that point and hold it for 2 minutes

Your head should feel much better after this.

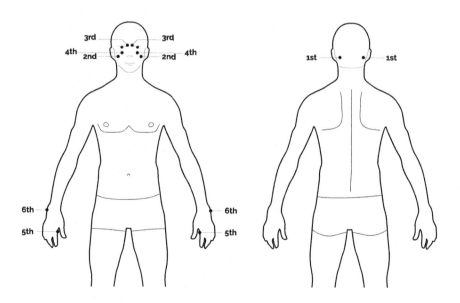

For headaches and migraines that are on one side more than another, hold these acupressure points on that side.

* Place one hand on same side AP2 as the headache
* Place the other hand over the pubic bone (midway between AP15s) and hold together for 2–3 minutes
* Move hand from the pubic bone to AP1 on same side and hold for 2–3 minutes
* Move hand from AP1 to AP5 on same side and hold for 2–3 minute
* Then move hand from AP5 to AP7 on same side, hold for 2–3 minutes

This also helps with digestion and bloating, so it's good for abdominal migraines too.

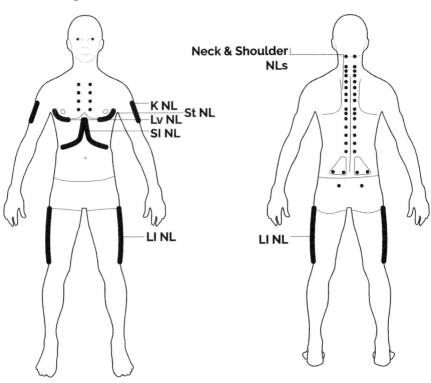

For over indulgence, migraine, hangover headaches and those that you think may be caused by overloading your system from rich food or alcohol. This helps stimulate the lymphatic reflexes of the liver to help it process the burden and aid detoxification. Plenty of water also helps.

* Rub the Lv NLs firmly along the right rib area where a bra wire would be, for about 30 seconds
* Hold acupressure points high 1s, to find these points, put the fingers of one hand on the inside of the knee on AP1 and allow the thumb to lightly stretch out along the inside of the thigh, where the thumb rests, is high 1
* Place both hands on high 1s for a few minutes
* Rub the LI NLs shown on the chart, massaging along the outer part of the thigh downwards and upwards, (please note you are not massaging the skin but the fleshy parts underneath) this can be quite sore

For headaches that occur as a storm brews, this can indicate that the build-up of positive ions created by those weather conditions are having an adverse effect. Try this to increase the negative ions and redress the balance.

* Close off your right nostril and breathe in through the left one
* Breathe out through the mouth
* Repeat several times

For these types of headaches, having a shower can help too. Have you noticed that when you stand near a waterfall how refreshing it feels? This is because the fast-flowing water creates more negative ions.

Neck tension headaches

It's worth looking at posture here, especially if you're at a desk staring at a screen for much of the day. As well as getting a break at regular intervals, try moving your head around every now and again so that the supporting muscles get a break.

FAST FIXES

Massaging the ears increases blood flow to brain, head, neck and shoulder area, increasing energy flow and flexibility whilst decreasing neck and shoulder tension.

It also stimulates all the acupuncture points on the ears (there is a whole mini acupuncture system on the ear).

Not only does it stimulate the acupuncture points and hence the energy flow in the body, it also helps the blood flow to the brain, helping get rid of "brain fog" as well as neck pain.

* Firmly massage the ears—all over the whole ear, inside and out, front and back

There are reflex areas on the thumb relating to the neck. Imagine the top of the thumb as the head and the area below the first joint as the neck.

* Massage the area around the base of the thumb covering all the area up to the first joint of the thumb

Headaches from eyestrain

If your eyes are having to work harder because they are tired, blood is diverted to the occipital region at the back of the brain which deals with vision. This is why you feel this type of headache at the back of the head. There is more information in the section on 'Eyes'.

FAST FIXES

To strengthen the eye muscles and take the strain off the brain, this can be done 2 or 3 times every day.

* Put your palm over the navel and with the thumb and 2 fingers of the other hand, rub the hollows under the collarbone, AP22s. Whilst keeping your head still, move your eyes to look up, down, to the left and then the right (a few seconds in each position)

* Then move them slowly to the left, slowly back and then over to the right, repeat 3 times

* Swap hands and repeat all of the above

* Now put your palm over the navel and with the thumb and 2 fingers of the other hand, rub the hollows under the collarbone, AP22s. While keeping your head still, move your eyes to look into the distance for a few seconds, then focus them on something quite close to you

* Swap hands and repeat

This last one is especially important now that we are using computers and smartphones much more. We are looking more and more at electromagnetic screens close to us and less and less into the distance.

You may find some of these eye movements difficult at first, but it will get easier and you will be able to move your eyes a bit further up, down, etc each time.

This helps (balance the blood sugar levels) to fuel the brain so it will function more efficiently.

* With your left arm by your side, find the point on your left ribcage where your elbow touches, put your hand there

* With your other hand, touch one of the AP22s

* Now tap both of these points together about 30 times

* Keeping your hand on the same point on your ribcage

* Move the other hand to the other AP22

* Repeat the tapping

Migraine

Migraine has many contributary factors including diet, gut health, liver health, stress, low blood sugar levels, food or environmental intolerances, bright or flickering lights, hormonal, emotional, physical or medicinal factors. It differs from a headache as it is often accompanied by severe pain, nausea, light and noise sensitivity and can last for days.

One client, a Deputy Head teacher, had very regular and debilitating migraines. Reflexology helped her so much, that after a number of treatments she only had the occasional episode. She also underwent a lot of medical and neurological tests to find out the cause and nothing was found. This was good news but at the same time, it didn't give her a reason as to why they occurred. We concluded it most likely was down to stress, although she wasn't totally convinced. A couple of months after this, being migraine free for a good length of time, the school got notice of an Ofsted inspection, she developed a migraine that very day! Now she had her answer.

Migraine can be linked to the digestive system and also the liver. It's worth looking through those sections too.

FAST FIXES

For over indulgence, migraine, hangover headaches and those that you think may be caused by overloading your system from rich food or alcohol, work on the Lv NLs.

These help to stimulate the lymphatic reflexes of the liver to help it process the burden and aid detoxification. Plenty of water also helps.

* Rub the Lv NLs firmly along the right rib area where a bra wire would be, for about 30 seconds

* Also rub the LI NLs shown on the chart, massaging along the outer part of the thigh downwards and upwards, (please note you are not massaging the skin but the fleshy parts underneath)–this can feel quite sore

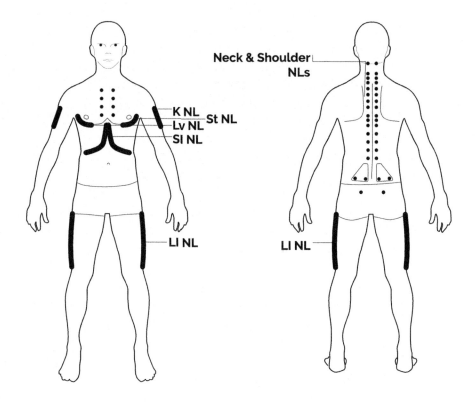

The acupressure points, high 1s are good to aid digestion. To find them put the fingers of one hand on the inside of the knee, AP1 and allow the thumb to lightly stretch up along the inside of the thigh, where the thumb rests, is high 1.

* Place both hands on high 1s for a few minutes

Hold these acupressure points for a few minutes on each set of points:

* Both AP4s together
* Both AP20s together
* Both AP21s together
* Both AP22s together

These points are also good for clearing the sinuses and bringing in AP4 helps encourage relaxation and sleep.

* Hold AP16 with same side AP5
* Swap sides and repeat

These 2 points are also good for pain in general.

Another pair of points which can help:

* Hold AP7 with same side AP12 for a few minutes
* Swap hands and repeat

When a migraine is severe try this:

* Cross the hands over and hold both AP7s together for a few minutes

With all of these repeat as often as is needed.

Eyes

It is said that only 10% of sight comes from the eyes, the rest of our vision comes from the brain making sense of what our eyes see and feed to the brain via the optic nerve.

Recent research[10] has shown that actually our eyes don't take in every detail, they get an overview of what is there and the brain fills in the gaps with what it expects from previous experience. Hence a chair shaped object becomes a chair.

This may explain why magicians can use distraction techniques to perform their magic. You are concentrating on what they are showing you—the pack of cards in their hand or the lady "being sawn in half". Elsewhere something else is happening, but because your focus isn't on that, your brain can ignore it and filter it out.

If you've ever watched Derren Brown, he has demonstrated this effect in various ways. In one show there was a guy playing table tennis when a man in a gorilla suit came on to the set and then walked off again, hardly anyone noticed! This is a prime example.

Our eyes and the brain need optimum blood sugar levels to function efficiently.

Hence nutrition (again) is very important. When complex carbohydrates (grains, starchy veg, pulses) are broken down in the body, they provide a steady stream of fuel as sugar, to enrich the blood and be converted into energy for the body. This is vital for the eyes and the brain to function well.

NB sugar itself or sugary foods, biscuits, cake, chocolate bars will just send a quick overload of sugar to the body which is quickly dealt with. The net effect is lower blood sugar levels than before and sending more signals to the brain for another quick fix of sugar. Coffee, tea and cigarettes will have a similar effect, raising blood sugar levels quickly due to stimulating the adrenal glands.

If our body is fatigued and low in energy, our vision will be affected, the eyes will not be able to focus on things properly, it may seem blurry, or we may feel dizzy and unfocused when we try to concentrate.

Computers can affect our electromagnetic field if we are feeling vulnerable, tired, hungry, dehydrated or stressed. It is time to take a break when your vision becomes blurry or unfocused.

FAST FIXES

For eyestrain:

* Hold the point AP4 on one side of the head
* With the other hand hold the AP21 on the opposite cheekbone
* Swap hands and repeat, 2–3 minutes each side

This can help when your eyes are tired:

* Put the fingers of your left hand onto AP19 in the right elbow
* Bend your right arm and place your hand over your right shoulder on AP3
* Hold together for 2–3 minutes
* Repeat on opposite side

Use as often as you like daily.

Cross-crawl exercise can help. This is basically marching or walking on the spot moving one arm and opposite leg at the same time in co-ordination, then doing the same with the other arm and opposite leg. Cross-crawl activates many different muscles in the body stimulating the connection between the right and left halves of the brain by forming more neural networks, so it is also a very powerful exercise to stimulate and improve brain function.

Marching on the spot improves your concentration, co-ordination, memory and lymph flow. Use cross-crawl to enhance brain function for vision.

* Cross-crawl slowly using exaggerated large movements for 30 seconds to 1 minute
* Repeat when needed

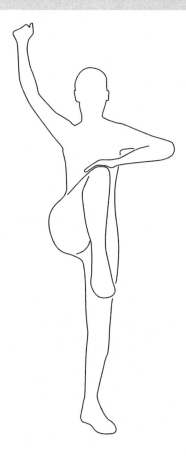

Now to strengthen the eye muscles and this can be done 2 or 3 times every day.

* Put your palm over the navel and with the thumb and 2 fingers of the other hand, rub the hollows under the collarbone, AP22s. While keeping the head still, move your eyes to look up, down, to the left and then the right (a few seconds in each position)
* Then move them slowly to the left, slowly back to centre and then over to the right, repeat 3 times
* Swap hands and repeat all of the above
* Put your palm over the navel and with the thumb and 2 fingers of the other hand, rub the hollows under the collarbone AP22s. Whilst keeping the head still, move your eyes to look into the distance for a few seconds then focus them on something quite close to you
* Swap hands and repeat

You may find some of these eye movements difficult at first, but it will get easier to move your eyes a bit further, up, down etc each time.

They are excellent for when your eyes are tired from close up work, reading and working on computers and will help improve concentration also.

* You can also massage the base of your index and middle fingers on the palm side of the hand, or the base of the 2nd and 3rd toes on the sole of the foot

These are reflex areas relating to the eyes.

Brain fog, memory & concentration

When our body is fatigued and low in energy, not only our vision will be affected, we may feel dizzy and unfocused when we try to concentrate.

Every day we are exposed to vast amounts of information, newspapers, TV, films, books, social media, magazines, internet searches. It's said that a daily edition of The Times newspaper contains more information than man (a few centuries ago), would be faced with in a lifetime! There is such bombardment on our consciousness these days, no wonder our memories fail us at times.

There are also hormonal influences, PMS, pregnancy, motherhood, the menopause and stress.

When trying to concentrate, there are distractions all the time, in the office from colleagues, the phone, emails pinging etc. This makes it hard for us to stay focused on the task in hand.

As mentioned before, computers can affect our electromagnetic field if we are feeling vulnerable, tired, hungry, dehydrated or stressed. The brain needs fuel for energy, water and oxygen to work well. When you start to feel spaced out, dizzy or unfocused, then it's best to have a break. You can use these techniques to give your brain and body an energy boost, so it can start to function efficiently again.

FAST FIXES

We have 14 meridians, two of which are central to the body (running up the front and up the back of the body). These act like storage batteries for the others. If these get depleted then our energy levels can drop. This simple exercise gives our Central meridian a quick energy boost.

* Run your hand a couple of inches above the body, along the path of the Central Meridian, which is upwards from the pubic bone to just below the bottom lip
* Repeat this 3 times but remember when you move your hand back to the start position, do this away from the body, so that you don't run the energy backwards!

Running this meridian will give a quick boost to your electro-magnetic reserves.

The same applies to drinking water. Water helps dilute the toxins so the kidneys can process them. There needs to be enough water in the body to allow this to happen, and if there isn't then the kidneys will take it from elsewhere in the body, including the brain. When the brain is dehydrated it can shrink in size, this can affect how well it functions.

Caffeine can also dehydrate the body, as the kidneys have to work harder to remove it.

* Drink a couple of glasses of water, then keep hydrated by drinking water throughout the day

Make drinking water a regular habit, rehydrating the body and brain can really make a difference to the clarity of our thinking processes.

Cross-crawl can help with concentration and brain fog. It is basically marching or walking on the spot moving one arm and the opposite leg at the same time in co-ordination, then doing the same with the other arm and the opposite leg. Cross-crawl activates many different muscles in the body stimulating the connection between the right and left halves of the brain by forming more neural networks, so it is also a very powerful exercise to stimulate and improve brain function.

Marching on the spot improves your concentration, co-ordination, memory and lymph flow. Cross-crawl movements also activate the speech and language centres of the brain.

* Cross-crawl slowly using exaggerated large movements for 30 seconds to 1 minute
* Repeat when needed

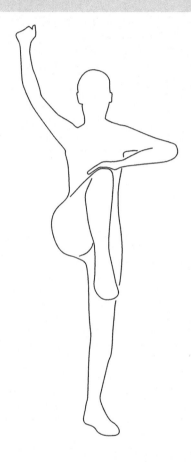

This also helps switch the brain back on, so we can think more clearly.

* Place the fingers and thumb of one hand around the navel and press them into the body
* With the thumb and 2 fingers of the other hand, rub the hollows under the collarbone, on the points AP22s

* Then move the thumb and 2 fingers to just above the top lip and below the bottom lip and rub these points too
* Swap hands and repeat

To help balance the blood sugar levels and fuel the brain so it will function more efficiently try this:

* With your left arm by your side find the point on your left ribcage where your elbow touches, put your right hand there
* With your left hand, touch one of the points AP22
* Now tap both of these points together about 30 times
* Keeping your right hand on the point on your ribcage
* Move your left hand to the other AP22
* Repeat the tapping

Releasing stress and anxiety if we are feeling overwhelmed can help too.

* Hold the AP20s on the forehead lightly, using 2 fingers of each hand and think about feeling overwhelmed and struggling to concentrate
* Then after a few minutes you can change those thoughts, visualising yourself feeling calmer, thinking more clearly and feeling more motivated

This technique brings the blood flow back to the front of the brain which helps us think clearly and rationally.

These easy exercises all help brain function and used long term can have a beneficial effect on improving memory too.

Ears

The outer part of the ear acts as "directional antennae" directing the sound through to the eardrum. Here the air resonates and activates the little bones inside the ear to produce sound waves that the tiny hairs pick up and waft along for the brain to interpret.

The brain can filter out sounds. Think about being in a crowded café, there is music playing, people talking, plus the sound of the coffee machines too. You're happily engrossed in chatting to a friend or reading a good book, not noticing the noise around you until something changes, either a new sound or a quietening, then you suddenly become aware of it.

Constant loud noise over a certain decibel level can affect hearing, leading to loss of quality of sound in varying degrees. Stress and noise can also affect the ears in the form of tinnitus.

Constant ear infections can lead to glue ear which inhibits the transmission of sound waves within the ear leading to muffled hearing. As the ear is virtually a closed system it is difficult for the infection and its by-products to dissipate away.

In Chinese Medicine, the ears relate to the body in foetus form and have a mini acupuncture system on them. Massaging firmly all over the outer part of the ears inside and outside, front and back, is like stimulating all those acupuncture points on the ear. It has an immediate effect on concentration, increasing alertness, helping hearing and vision, as well as having a noticeable effect on neck pain.

Dizziness, imbalance and vertigo can be related to problems within the ear. The semi-circular canals inside the ear, affect our balance and the way we perceive the outside world. The brain then relates this information to the information it is getting from the eyes. If these two pieces of information don't correspond, our body gets distressed, we feel dizzy, disorientated and unbalanced. There can also be nausea, hence why we get sea sickness. The swaying horizon doesn't correspond with the fact that we are standing on a stable surface and not perceiving movement until we look towards the horizon.

FAST FIXES

These two exercises are very helpful for balance. They help centre us and cope with the effects of gravity, so they can take away the strain of holding ourselves upright.

They are also good for back problems.

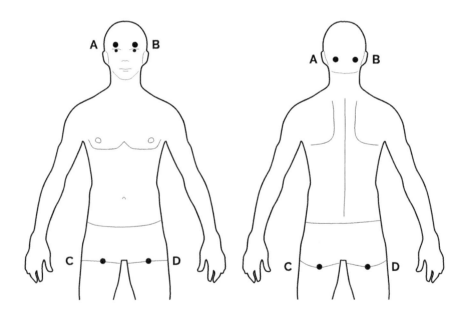

There are 4 pairs of points involved, 2 pairs on the front of the body and 2 pairs on the back. You will be holding one of the head points with one of the lower ones each time.

On the front of the body:

* Touch point A above the eyebrow and contact point C, hold together for up to a minute (A&C)
* Keeping your fingers on A, move the other hand to point D and hold both points for up to a minute (A&D)
* Now move the hand above the eyebrow to the point B and hold with D for up to a minute (B&D)
* Move the lower hand onto C and hold both points for up to a minute (C&D)

This next part uses points on the back of the head, between the back of the ear and the neck and the points on your sitting bone.

* Touch point A on the back of the head and contact point C, hold for up to a minute (A&C)
* Keeping your fingers on A, move the other hand to point D and hold both points for up to a minute (A&D)
* Now move the hand on the back of the head to point B and hold with D for up to a minute (B&D)
* Move the lower hand over to C and hold both points for up to a minute (C&D)

Repeat as needed.

This stimulates all the acupuncture points on the ears, helping us to focus on what is being said.

* Firmly massage the ears, all over the whole ear, inside and out, back and front

Use any of the following for ear issues:

* Hold both the AP14s for 2–3 minutes

* Hold the points AP11 and AP25 on the same side for 2–3 minutes

* Hold the points AP4 and AP21 on opposite sides for 2–3 minutes

* Hold the acupressure point CX 6 on both wrists

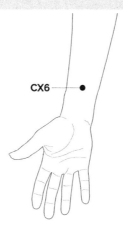

CX6

This last one is great for motion sickness too.

This flow has been known to help with all sorts of issues to do with the ears, hearing, ringing and earache for example.

* Hold both of the points AP20s together for 2–3 minutes
* Hold both of the points AP21s together for 2–3 minutes
* Hold both of the points AP22s together for 2–3 minutes

For ringing in the ears, doing this is said to help:

* Hold the ring finger on the side that's affected, if it's both do both hands

Ear infections can be helped by drinking water, taking probiotics (to help reduce candida infections caused by continuous antibiotics), cutting out sugar and also working on the Eustachian tube reflexes on the hand (see below). The Eustachian tube runs from the ear to the throat and if it's congested it doesn't allow waste to drain away from the ear.

Yawning helps unblock this and balance out the air pressure between the inner ear and the atmosphere (as you will know when taking off or landing in an aeroplane or just driving up and down hilly mountain roads).

* Rubbing the point at the web between middle and ring fingers on the palm side
* Rub along the base of the ring and little fingers

These will often be very sore if there is congestion, but also quick to relieve congestion when worked on intermittently over the day. I would do this for my children during take-off and landing when flying.

You can use these points quite often throughout the day for an acute infection.

* Hold the points AP4 and AP21 on opposite sides for 2–3 minutes
* Swap sides and repeat

If you have longer this can work well and will help other problems too.

* Place your right hand on left side AP12
* Place your left hand on left side AP13
* Hold for 2–3 minutes
* Move your left hand onto left side AP15
* Hold for 2–3 minutes

* Move your left hand onto left side AP1
* Hold for 2–3 minutes
* Swap hands to the other side and repeat

If the infection is just in one ear, use the points on that side only.

Sinuses

Sinusitis, sinus congestion, rhinitis seems more prevalent in today's western world. The sinuses are empty cavities in the spaces in the skull behind the cheeks and forehead.

A runny nose after eating is often indicative of a possible intolerance to some part of that meal (like when you sneeze in a dusty room). Wheat, sugar, milk, tea, coffee and chocolate are all common culprits.

Intolerances, as opposed to allergies, stem from the body being over-loaded with a certain food and not being able to process it properly. Certain ingredients are much more common in processed foodstuffs than they ever were 20 years ago. For instance, sugar is in many more foods now even basic breakfast cereals.

Low fat usually means more sugar and modified starch (usually corn). Wheat appears in many foods (it's often found now even in crisps, which used to contain just potatoes, oil and salt) and manufactured ready meals.

Salt intake can be high if we eat a lot of processed food. MSG and yeast are often used as flavour enhancers too.

If our bodies are having problems processing these foods easily then the constant overload means our bodies are overstretched and constantly dealing with the effects. Hence, we may get the mucous response in the sinuses leading to sinus drip or congestion. IBS, feeling tired, slight hangover feeling, skin problems, achy joints or generally feeling under par, can all be indications of food intolerances.

The good news is that the sinuses will respond very quickly to intervention, often releasing the mucous fairly quickly.

Identifying and avoiding any stressful foods will help, there are various ways to do this, including kinesiology.

FAST FIXES

Facial reflex and acupressure points that will help:

* Using the middle fingers press gently, starting at the inner corner of the eyebrows and moving slowly along the bony parts of the eye sockets around the eye, until you reach the start point
* Press the points at the inner corner of the eyebrows for 5—10 seconds
* Press the points next to the nose, halfway down the nose for 5—10 seconds
* Press the points next to the nose, at the bottom of the nose for 5—10 seconds
* Do all of this sequence three times

The fingers and toes are reflexes for the sinuses.

* Massage all along each of the fingers or toes

Toes are easier as there is less area to work on, although fingers are more accessible.

This sequence is great for headaches and ear problems, as well as sinuses.

* Hold both of the AP20s together for 2–3 minutes
* Hold both of the AP21s together for 2–3 minutes
* Hold both of the AP22s together for 2–3 minutes

This helps if there is infection there too.

* Hold the points AP3 and AP15 together on the same side together for 2–3 minutes

If all of your head feels stuffy and blocked, try this one:

* Hold the points AP4 and AP21 on opposite sides

This can help get the ICV functioning better, which can have a beneficial effect on the sinuses too.

*Hold the following sets of points in pairs on the **right** side of the body, for about 30 seconds on each set.*

* Along inner edge of foot and inner ankle (1 on the chart)
* 2 inches above inner ankle and on wrist just below the thumb (2 on the chart)
* Halfway along a diagonal line from the navel to hip/ top of thigh and the hollow just below the clavicle (3 on the chart)
* Rub the NLs downwards and upwards a few times, massaging along the outer part of the thigh, please note you are not massaging the skin but the fleshy parts underneath–this can be quite painful
* If you have longer then also hold the NVs on either side of the head above the ears on the ridge for up to a minute

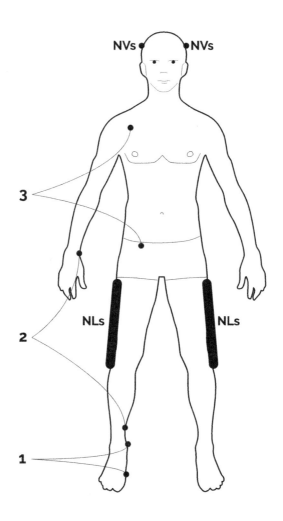

Frozen shoulder

The shoulder joint is a very shallow joint (unlike the hip which is a ball and socket joint). The bones are held in place by the muscles and ligaments. This means that if one of the muscles attached to these bones becomes strained, inflamed or injured and doesn't get chance to heal, the other muscles around that joint can start to compensate for the injured muscle. They can then in turn become strained or over used. When this happens, because more muscles around the joint are not functioning as they should, their range of movement becomes limited and painful too. Hence the term frozen shoulder!

The aim is to get these muscles switched back on and truly functioning again so that there is full movement in that joint.

FAST FIXES

Move the arm around, gently, so you can feel the tight and painful areas before you start.

* Touch both AP20s with your thumb and 2 fingers of the one hand
* Place the thumb and finger tips of the other hand around your navel
* Keeping the hand on the forehead still, push in with the fingers of the other hand and stimulate with a circular motion for about 30 seconds
* Now put your thumb pads onto the nail of your index fingers
* Keeping your thumbs in this position, touch both AP20s on the forehead with the middle and ring fingers for about a minute

* Visualise those muscles that feel tight, relaxing and
  feeling much easier, for about a minute

*Again, move the affected area around, gently, so you can feel the
improvement. You can repeat this as often as you like.*

Move the arm around, gently so you can feel the tight and painful areas before you start.

Rubbing the neurolymphatic points for some of the shoulder muscles can help the lymph flow drain toxins from these muscles, which will help free them up again.

* Rub the NLs situated either side of the sternum on the front of the body in the rib spaces just below the collarbones and the ones below those too
* Also rub the points on the back either side of the spine (never rub on the spine directly) just down from the big knobbly bone at the base of the neck and the ones below that to the level of the bottom of the shoulder blade

Now move the arm around gently again and notice the difference in movement and comfort.

All of these will help, but because of the slightly different way each works, you will probably find one (or more) that works best for you. Why not give them all a try!

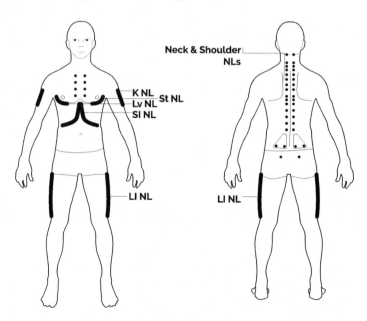

Back problems

Back pain is the biggest cause of ill health in the world. A major international study[11] (analysis of 188 countries) has found that back pain causes more ill health than any other condition. And of this, lower back pain is most predominant. Neck pain takes second place in England and Scotland.

Backache appears to be occurring much earlier in life with nearly half of under thirties having back problems. We are much less active than we used to be, with both children and adults spending more time hunched over tablets and mobiles.

The back is our support mechanism, a precise alignment of bones and muscles that allows us to stay upright. The co-ordination involved in keeping this structure balanced and flexible is massive. From carrying a bag on one shoulder, bending down to pick up something we've dropped, to carrying children, our back supports us through all of this without us even thinking about it, until suddenly it doesn't function properly. Back problems creep up on us as strain on the muscles and possibly nutritional deficiencies all take their toll.

Back problems seem to "reverberate" up and down the spine over time. So, for instance a whiplash injury to the neck, when eventually clearing up can then manifest as a lower back problem. This in turn can later show up again as a neck problem. Helping these problems when they first start to show up can prevent future problems elsewhere.

Injury to the neck muscles will, as they struggle to heal, have an impact on nearby muscles, resulting in them having to help support the injured neck ones. These support muscles can then become overtired, so this makes them rely on other muscles in the area. In the end the whole structure stiffens and locks up causing pain and immobility. This puts pressure on the vertebrae which can impinge on vulnerable disc tissue, this can then affect the nerves in the spinal cord, causing great pain.

Using some of the techniques here will allow the muscles to function better and relieve the pressure on other muscles and bones, bringing back movement and flexibility.

Try lengthening your spine. Being careful not to arch your back, take a deep breath in and feel as though you are growing taller. Then maintain that height as you exhale. Repeat the breathing in, grow even taller and maintain that new height as you exhale. Do this regularly and frequently to help to strengthen your abdominal muscles, so they can help support the back muscles which helps alleviate pain.

You can also do shoulder rolls, gently pull your shoulders up, push them back and then let them drop to open up the chest and take a deep breath to stretch and lengthen the spine.

FAST FIXES

For pain in any area of the back

Be aware of which areas feel uncomfortable or painful before you start.

* Touch the points AP20s with your thumb and 2 fingers of one hand
* Place the thumb and finger tips of the other hand round your navel
* Whilst keeping the hand on the forehead still, push in with the fingers of the other hand and stimulate with a circular motion for about 30 seconds
* Now put your thumb pads onto the nail of your index fingers
* Keeping your thumbs in this position, touch the AP20s on the forehead with your middle and ring fingers for about a minute
* Visualise those muscles that feel tight, relaxing and feeling much easier

Now be aware of the changes in those areas so you can feel the improvement.

You can follow up with this exercise:

* Place your thumb and index finger pads together
* Then put your middle finger onto your index fingernail
* Using these fingers touch the AP20s on the forehead for a couple of minutes
* Visualise your back and those muscles that feel tight, relaxing and feeling much easier

You can repeat any of these as often as you like. You may find one of them more effective than the others.

A client with sciatica had pain from her lower back all the way down her leg. Using these exercises, the pain reduced to one small area in the lower back, and the muscles felt much more relaxed and easier overall.

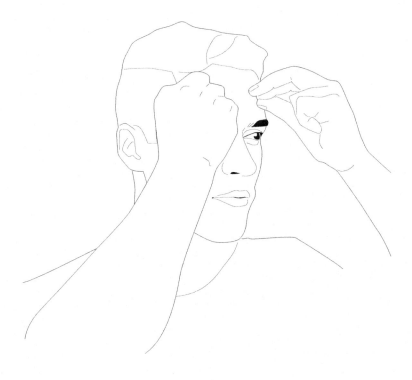

These next 2 exercises are also good for back problems. They help centre us and cope with the effects of gravity, so they can take away the strain of holding ourselves upright.

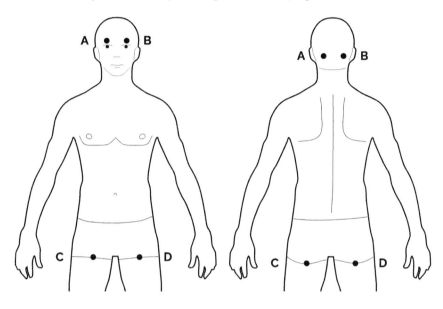

There are 4 pairs of points involved, 2 pairs on the front of the body and 2 pairs on the back. You will be holding one of the head points with one of the lower ones each time.

On the front of the body:

* Touch point A above the eyebrow and contact point C, hold together for up to a minute (A&C)

* Keeping your fingers on A, move the other hand to point D and hold both points for up to a minute (A&D)

* Now move the hand above the eyebrow to the point B and hold with D for up to a minute (B&D)

* Move the lower hand onto C and hold both points for up to a minute (C&D)

This next part uses points on the back of the head, between the back of the ear and the neck and the points on your sitting bone.

* Touch point A on the back of the head and contact point C, hold for up to a minute (A&C)
* Keeping your fingers on A, move the other hand to point D and hold both points for up to a minute (A&D)
* Now move the hand on the back of the head to point B and hold with D for up to a minute (B&D)
* Move the lower hand over to C and hold both points for up to a minute (C&D)

Repeat as needed.

*The **Main Central Vertical Energy** Flow is the deepest energy flow in the body and very beneficial for anyone who has chronic illnesses. It is great for helping the back, the spine, the spinal cord and the nervous system, the digestive system, the chakras and the meridian energies. I like to think it re aligns our whole system.*

For more information on how this can help you, please go the section on 'Preventative Health'.

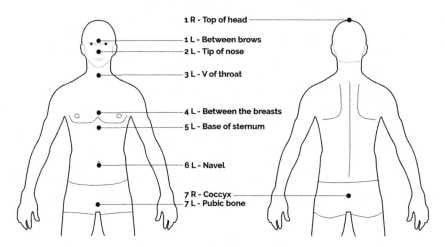

1 R - Top of head
1 L - Between brows
2 L - Tip of nose
3 L - V of throat
4 L - Between the breasts
5 L - Base of sternum
6 L - Navel
7 R - Coccyx
7 L - Pubic bone

* Place your right hand on the top of your head, this remains there until the last step
* Place your left middle finger on the third eye (between the eyebrows) for 2–3 minutes
* Move your left middle finger to the tip of nose, hold for 2–3 minutes
* Move your left middle finger to the "V" of the throat, hold for 2–3 minutes
* Move your left middle finger to the sternum, between the breasts, hold for 2–3 minutes
* Move your left middle finger to the base of sternum (solar plexus) hold for 2–3 minutes
* Move your left middle finger to the navel, hold for 2–3 minutes
* Move your left middle finger to the centre of the pubic bone, hold for 2–3 minutes
* Move your right hand (palm side or back) onto the coccyx, keeping your left hand on the pubic bone. Hold these points for 2–3 minutes

It will probably take you 15–20 minutes, but you can do this whilst reading, watching TV, or lying in the bath if you like.

Neck

Most people will have experienced neck ache at some point, usually due to sleeping in an awkward position, bad posture or injury.

These days staring at a screen for much of the day can cause problems with the neck and shoulders, so it's worth taking a break at regular intervals and moving your head around every now and again to ease the supporting muscles.

FAST FIXES

Massaging the ears increases the blood flow to brain, neck and shoulder area, increasing energy flow and flexibility whilst decreasing neck and shoulder tension.

It also stimulates all the acupuncture points on the ears (there is a whole mini acupuncture system on the ear). Not only does it stimulate the acupuncture points and hence the energy flow in the body, it also helps the blood flow to the brain, helping get rid of "brain fog" as well as neck pain.

Move your head and neck around so you can feel the tight and painful areas before you start.

* Firmly massage both ears—all over the whole ear, inside and out, back and front

You should find that turning the head now feels a lot easier and the head moves further to the side. If you would like to increase the flexibility further:

* Turn your head as far as it will go comfortably and massage the ears as before
* Now turn your head to the other side as far as it will go comfortably and massage the ears as before

This should ease it off even more.

It also has a noticeable effect on concentration, increasing alertness, helping hearing and vision, as well as having an immediate effect on neck pain.

When giving talks in the past I have often used this technique to demonstrate how quickly kinesiology can work. Getting a volunteer with neck pain to turn their head as far as is comfortable, giving their ears a firm rub, then repeating the head turning, it is so noticeable for both the volunteer and the audience that there has been a huge change in the range of movement and decrease in pain. A true "aha" moment!

Almost everyone has neck problems at some point, so this is a valuable tip to remember.

This technique helps muscles that seem frozen, often quite common when attempting to move the head. Move your head and neck around so you can feel the tight and painful areas before you start.

* Put your thumb pads onto the nail of your index fingers
* Keeping your thumbs in this position, touch both points AP20s on the forehead with your middle and ring fingers for about a minute
* Visualise those muscles that feel tight, relaxing and the movement feeling much easier, do this for about a minute

When moving your head and neck afterwards you will notice the benefit immediately. You can repeat this as often as you like.

There are reflex areas on the thumb relating to the neck. Imagine the top of the thumb as the head and the area under the joint as the neck.

* Massage the area around the base of the thumb up to and around the first joint of the thumb

This helps the blood and lymph flow to the neck muscles, so they become less tight.

* Hold the points AP11 and opposite side AP12 for a few minutes and then swap over

Mid area of the back (from shoulder to waist)

This area can be stiff and hold a lot of tension again due to poor posture. Muscle strain from lifting heavy objects can cause problems here too.

FAST FIXES

Rubbing the neurolymphatic points for some of the shoulder muscles can help the lymph flow drain toxins from these muscles which will help free them up again.

* Firmly rub these points that are situated either side of the sternum on the front of the body, in the rib spaces just below the collarbones and the ones below those too
* Also rub the points on the back either side of the spine (never rub on the spine directly) just down from the big knobbly bone at the base of the neck and the ones below down to the bottom of the shoulder blade

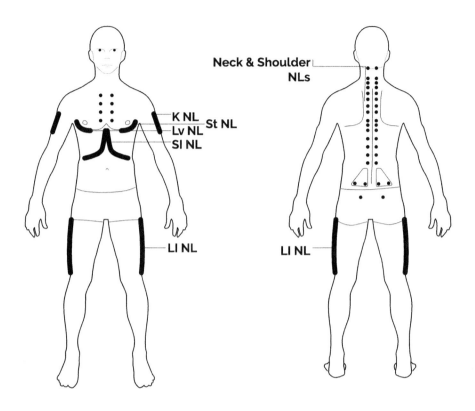

Neck & Shoulder
NLs

K NL
St NL
Lv NL
SI NL

LI NL

LI NL

Use this neurovascular point to help bring back the blood flow to the shoulder area. It's worth making the arm movements (not to excess) that are painful as you do this and as you continue to hold the point, you'll find the range of movement will increase.

* Hold the point on top of the head, where a baby's soft spot would be for about 30 seconds to a minute–you can find this by placing the heel of your hand between the eyebrows, and the point is where the tip of your middle finger touches the top of your head

Some time ago I met someone with Chronic Fatigue Syndrome, she was in a really bad place, not able to walk and spent most of the time in bed or a wheelchair due to the debilitating fatigue.

When we first met and talked, she couldn't even lift her arm from the controls of her chair. I held this point on her head for a few minutes and she found that she could move her arms, in her words "they were going like windmills!"

Her mum brought her to me for treatment and after 3 or 4 sessions, she actually walked from the car into the house! We both had a moment...

She carried on coming at regular intervals and her health improved so much that she learned to drive and was able to start living life again.

I think this really illustrates how doing small things regularly and consistently can lead to big improvements.

Holding the following acupuncture points, bilaterally, simultaneously and in the order shown below will help with pain around the neck and shoulders.

As these points are on the hands and arms, you have to find your own way of using your fingers and thumbs to be able to contact these points so that it is comfortable for you.

* Touch both acu points H 3 using your fingers/thumbs and hold for a minute or two
* Touch both acu points LI 4 using your fingers/thumbs and hold for a minute or two
* Touch both acu points LI 11 using your fingers/thumbs and hold for a minute or two
* Touch both acu points LI 15 using your fingers/thumbs and hold for a minute or two

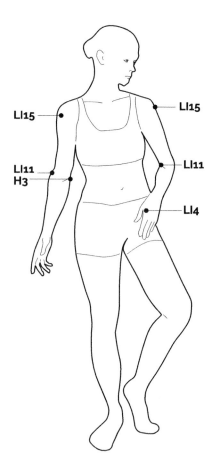

This is a great one to use every day:

* Start with putting one hand on point AP25 on your sitting bone
* The other hand goes over your shoulder on the same side of the body on point AP11
* Hold these points for a few minutes
* Then move your hand from AP25 to AP15 at the front of the body, keeping your other hand on AP11, again hold these points for a few minutes

> * Swap sides and repeat, it should take you less than 10 minutes

You can do this every day and more than once in the day as well.

More acupressure points that will help:

> * You can hold both AP19s for a few minutes

There are reflex areas on the hands relating to the back. Imagine the area from the 1st to the 2nd joint of the thumb as the neck and the area from the joint to the wrist, as the back.

> * Massage along the side of your hand from the 2nd joint of the thumb down towards the wrist and back up again a few times, massaging more where it feels tender

Lower back (waist to tailbone)

Pain in this area can be attributed to a sprain or strain, a prolapsed disc or irritation of the sciatic nerve. Although quite often there appears to be no apparent cause.

Looking at posture, regular exercise and back exercises can all help. Changing your mattress can often help too, I have seen the benefit of this for a number of clients.

FAST FIXES

> * Start with putting one hand on point AP25 on your sitting bone
> * The other hand goes over your shoulder on the same side of the body on point AP11
> * Hold these points for a few minutes
> * Then move your hand from AP25 to AP15 at the front of the body, keeping your other hand on AP11, again hold these points for a few minutes

* Swap sides and repeat, it should take you less than 10 minutes

You can do this every day and more than once in the day as well.

The points AP2 and AP1 are really helpful for lower back, hip and upper leg problems.

* Place one hand on AP1
* Place the other hand on AP2 on the same side
* Hold them together for a few minutes and then swap sides

Or you can use the same points in a slightly different way, go with which feels the best for you:

* Place one hand on AP1
* Place the other hand on AP2 on the opposite side
* Hold them together for a few minutes and then swap sides

Repeat as often as you like during the day.

The next points help increase the lymphatic drainage of the muscles in the lower back, increasing circulation and removal of toxins, allowing tense muscles to relax.

For lower back pain and sciatica:

* Firmly massage the areas that are shaded on the chart

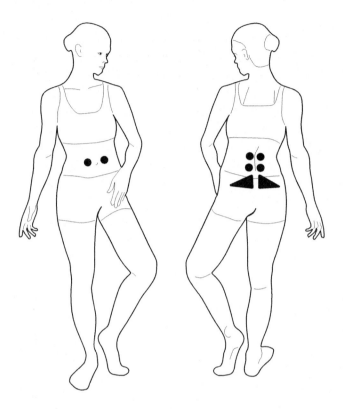

There are reflex areas on the hands relating to the back. Imagine the 2nd joint of the thumb as the neck and the area from that joint to the base of the hand where it meets the wrist as the back.

* Massage the area along the side of the hand from the 2nd joint of the thumb down to the wrist and back up again a few times

* Also massage the area of the wrist at the base of the hand below the little finger

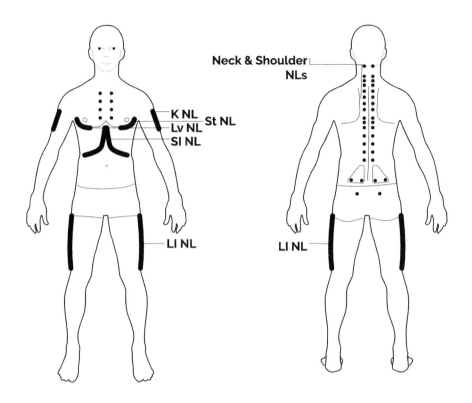

To keep the whole of the spine healthy, rub all the NLs on the back of the body. You will probably need someone else to help massage the points on the upper part of the back.

This has an effect on all the body organs as well as spinal nerves.

If there is a lot of pain:

* Hold the points AP16 and AP5 on the affected side (or both sides) for a few minutes

This can also help with pain in general.

Backache and sciatica

The sciatic nerve branches from your lower back through your hips and buttocks and down each leg. When there is pressure on the nerve, usually caused by a prolapsed disc, pain can radiate anywhere along its path. Sciatica tends to affect only one side of the body.

FAST FIXES

For lower back pain and sciatica:

> * Firmly massage the areas that are shaded on the chart

These can feel very sore, but it can bring instant relief for lower back and leg pain.

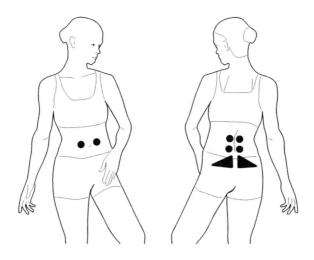

This helps back pain in general and also works well for sciatic pain.

> * Start with putting one hand on point AP25 on your sitting bone
> * The other hand goes over your shoulder on the same side of the body on point AP11
> * Hold these points for a few minutes

* Then move your hand from AP25 to AP15 at the front of the body, keeping your other hand on AP11, again hold these points for a few minutes

* Swap sides and repeat, it should take you less than 10 minutes

You can do this as often as you like during the day and every day too.

Arthritis

There are 2 forms of arthritis, osteo and rheumatoid. Osteo is due to wear and tear on the joints and rheumatoid is inflammatory. Both forms can result in very painful joints.

FAST FIXES

These points can help with pain, use as often as you like every day.

* Hold both points AP5 and AP16 on the same foot for 2–3 minutes
* Hold the points on the other foot for a few minutes

To help flush out accumulated toxins:

* Touch the painful joint and at the same time hold AP11 on the same side as the affected joint for a few minutes
* Still touching the painful area swap to the opposite side AP11

This is great for helping to increase our general body range of motion.

* Tap firmly with the fingertips all over the front, back and sides of the ribcage

Test the movement of the affected joint before and after and notice the difference. One client found this particularly helpful for his shoulder, he could move his arm further outwards and upwards after doing this.

For pain and stiffness in joints.

* Put the fingers of your left hand onto AP19 in the right elbow
* Bend your right arm and place your hand over your right shoulder on AP3
* Hold together for 2–3 minutes
* Repeat on opposite side

Use as often as you like daily.

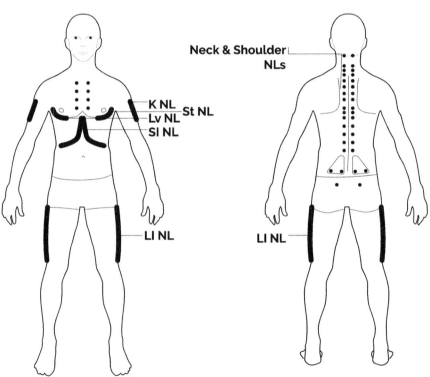

* You can also touch the affected area and at the same time rub firmly along the outer side of the thighs from hipbone to knee (the area labelled LI NLs) making sure you are massaging the flesh underneath the skin

This can often be quite sore!

Try moving the joint gently, so you can feel the tight and painful areas before you start.

* Touch the AP20s with your thumb and 2 fingers of the other hand
* Place the thumb and finger tips of one hand round your navel
* Whilst keeping the hand on the forehead still, push in with the fingers of the other hand and stimulate with a circular motion for about 30 seconds
* Next put your thumb pads onto the nail of your index fingers
* Keeping your thumbs in this position, touch the AP20s on the forehead with middle and ring fingers of both hands for about a minute
* Visualise those muscles and areas that feel tight, relaxing and feeling much easier, do this for about a minute

Again, move the affected area around, gently, so you can feel the improvement.

You can repeat this as often as you like.

In reflexology there are cross reflexes and we use these when an area is too painful or swollen to touch. The elbows are cross reflexes for the knees.

* Massage all around the elbow back and front on the same side as the painful knee
* For both knees do both elbows

You will be surprised how painful this can be!

I had a client who was due to have a knee operation, every time he came for reflexology I worked on his elbow. His knee felt much better, so he cancelled the operation.

For knees:

* Hold point AP1 on the same side as the sore knee together with the AP26 on the opposite side for a few minutes
* If it's both knees, swap sides

Another set of points for knees:

* Holding points AP8 and AP11 both on the same side for 2–3 minutes, can be beneficial too

For knees and hips:

* Hold same side the AP1 with AP2 for a few minutes, then swap sides

For neck and shoulders:

* Hold AP11 with the opposite side AP13 for a few minutes
* Swap sides and repeat

For feet and ankles:

* Hold AP5 with the same side AP1 for a few minutes
* Swap sides and repeat

When an area is very painful use these points:

* Hold both points AP5 and AP16 on the same foot for 2–3 minutes
* Swap sides and repeat

Remember:

* If the problem, pain or inflammation is on the right side—treat the right side
* If the problem, pain or inflammation is on the left side—treat the left side
* If the problem is in the present, if you are aware of what may be causing it, or if a male energy is involved, then treat the right side
* If the problem is from the past, if you don't know why it has happened, or if a female energy is involved, then treat the left side
* Use your intuition, whichever side you instinctively choose
* If in doubt do the right side first to clear the present, then the left to clear the past

Here are more cross reflexes. When an area is painful and sore, rather than massage that area directly which may not be beneficial, you can massage the corresponding cross reflex. For painful toes, you can massage the corresponding fingers. If the big toe and second toe on the left foot are sore then you would massage the thumb and index finger on the left hand for example.

* For toes—massage the corresponding fingers
* For fingers—massage the corresponding toes
* For wrists—massage the corresponding ankle
* For ankles—massage the corresponding wrist
* For elbows—massage the corresponding knee
* For knees—massage the corresponding elbow

This is great to do if you sprain your ankle, put your feet up and massage around your wrist every so often.

Digestive problems

When we are under stress, on medication, have had antibiotics, or there is alcohol and sugar in the diet, this can create the ideal conditions for food intolerances and digestive issues to develop.

Normal everyday foods become difficult for the body to process properly, so they end up triggering an immune response and the body tries to fight them off instead of treating them as nutrients.

It can be difficult to discover the guilty foods as the degree of intolerance varies due to the amount of stress the body is under, how much you eat of that particular food, how you are feeling, even the time of day can make a difference!

Common food intolerances are wheat (there is much more gluten in modern day wheat), milk, cheese, tea, coffee, chocolate and people with joint problems can be sensitive to potatoes, tomatoes, peppers and aubergines (all members of the nightshade family).

Kinesiology can help discover if certain foods are causing you problems and also help bring the body back into good working order so that they no longer affect you.

I have seen clients achieve remarkable results with this process as it addresses many different factors that can contribute and the bonus is that you lose weight!

When I tested one lady for food intolerances, she said I had just described the entire contents of her fridge, she changed what she ate and lost 10 lbs in 10 days!

Gastric reflux, indigestion & heartburn

We've probably all suffered from indigestion at some time. That awful feeling of being too full and the heartburn that accompanies it.

For some people this is an everyday state of affairs and if left untreated, it can develop into a much more serious problem.

Over eating, food intolerances or the "wrong" foods can be an issue. Problems further down the digestive tract can contribute too, there can be many factors involved with gastric reflux.

Kinesiology really helps here as it looks at the whole of the body and determines which is the best way forward.

FAST FIXES

These two techniques have helped many of my clients with digestive issues and I would recommend doing both of them in this order:

* Put one hand on the top of your head where a baby's soft spot would be–you can find this by placing the heel of your hand between the eyebrows, and the point is where the tip of your middle finger touches the top of your head

* Then rub firmly and quite slowly all along the sternum from the top to the bottom and back up again a few times

This helps tone the diaphragm which sits around the top of the stomach where the junction with the oesophagus is.

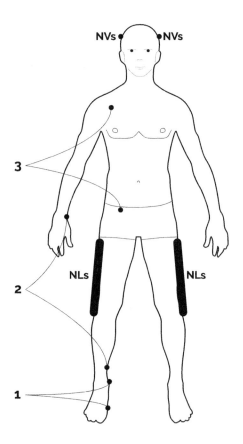

To help get the ICV and the whole of the digestive tract functioning better, hold the following sets of points in pairs on the right side of the body only, for 30 seconds on each set.

* Along inner edge of foot and inner ankle (1 on the chart)
* 2 inches above inner ankle and on wrist just below the thumb (2 on the chart)
* Halfway along a diagonal line from navel to hip/top of thigh and the hollow just below the clavicle (3 on the chart)
* Rub the NLs, shaded areas on chart, downwards and upwards a few times, massaging along the outer part of

the thigh, please note you are not massaging the skin but the fleshy parts underneath–this can be quite painful

* If you have longer then also hold the NVs on either side of the head above the ears on the bony ridge for up to a minute

Constipation & Diarrhoea

A bowel movement every day, usually in the morning, is classed as normal.

The digestive system really consists of a very long tube connected by valves which open and close to allow the food to pass though the body to be processed and absorbed and the remainder eliminated. When you think that most people tend to eat three times a day, then it would probably make more sense to have a bowel movement three times a day. Look at babies or animals, they tend to eliminate after each meal. Obviously, this wouldn't be convenient for most adults, so one movement a day preferably in the morning makes sense.

For a lot of folks however, this doesn't happen and I have known clients who have only had a bowel movement every 2 or 3 days and in one very extreme case every 10 days.

Diarrhoea can be a response to something we've eaten, either a food that we are intolerant too or something that has gone off. The body wants to be rid of it quickly before it gets absorbed and causes problems elsewhere in the body. This is a normal reaction and will usually sort itself out fairly quickly.

But for many reasons, diarrhoea can be an everyday state for some people, with the urgency that can accompany it causing them huge problems.

Diet can make a huge difference, as can a good probiotic. And because there is a very strong link between the emotions and the gut, reducing stress can help and vice versa, helping the gut can have a very beneficial effect on our emotions, lowering anxiety levels. Getting your digestive system in order can help so much with mood. See the section on 'The Vagus Nerve' for more about this.

For many years I have been emphasising to clients about the importance of good bacteria in gut health and overall health too. They can help reduce inflammation, help your immune system, keep your blood sugar levels balanced, sleep well and even help you lose weight!

There are lots of foods that help increase and sustain the good bacteria in your gut, taking a probiotic supplement too is a quick and easy way to top them up.

Things that deplete your good bacteria are, sugar, tea and coffee, alcohol, stress, medication, antibiotics, smoking and a diet with a lot of processed food in it.

There is now lots of information and scientifically backed evidence, to substantiate all of this. A great read is The Psychobiotic Revolution by Scott C Anderson and also Mad Diet by Suzanne Lockhart.

FAST FIXES

For constipation try this:

* Rub the NLs in a downward motion a few times, massaging along the outer part of the thigh, please note you are not massaging the skin but the fleshy parts underneath–these areas can be quite sore
* If you have longer then also hold the NVs on either side of the head above the ears on the ridge for 30 seconds to a minute

Holding the following sets of points in pairs on the left side of the body only, for 30 seconds on each set, will also help.

* Along inner edge of foot and inner ankle (1 on the chart)

* 2 inches above inner ankle and on wrist just below the thumb (2 on the chart)
* Halfway along a diagonal line from the navel to hip/top of thigh and the hollow just below the clavicle (3 on the chart)

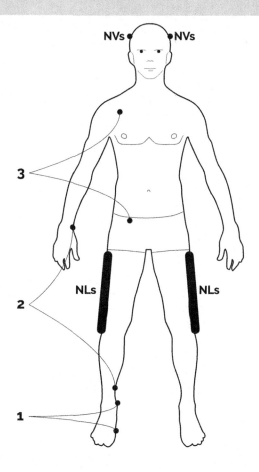

Another method for constipation:

* Touch AP8 on the left side with your left hand
* Touch AP11 on the left side with your right hand
* Hold together for 2–3 minutes
* Repeat as many times as you like during the day

Or you can use this sequence:

* Touch AP8 on the left side with your left hand
* Touch AP2 on the right side with your right hand
* Hold together for 2–3 minutes
* Repeat as many times as you like during the day

I have often given my clients "toilet training", with the aim of going to the loo every day at the same time.

They choose the best time for them and sit on the loo. They then put their hands over the lower point numbered 3 on the ICV chart (halfway between the navel and the hip joint on the right side of the body) and keep them there whilst sitting on the loo. Then they put their feet on a small stool (or a couple of books) so their lower legs are raised slightly and they are mimicking a squatting position. The stool puts the lower part of the large intestine into a straighter position meaning that gravity helps and there is less strain. Doing this every day helps reprogramme the bowel into a daily habit.

In our bathroom we have a small kiddie stool for anyone to use to get them into the optimum position for easy passage, my husband calls it "the stool stool".

Constipation, diarrhoea, IBS, colitis and other digestive disorders can be helped by working on the ileo-caecal valve (ICV).

The ICV is situated at the junction of the small intestine where it meets the large intestine. It is hugely important for the smooth functioning of the whole digestive system, and should open when food waste passes from the small intestine to the large bowel, then close. If it stays open, then toxins can leak back into the small intestine and be absorbed into the body, contributing to many issues. If it stays closed, then stagnation can also cause problems.

Having the ICV working properly is important for helping to resolve many symptoms in the body such as:

Headaches, migraines, stiff neck, shoulder pain, elbow pain, sudden thirst, indigestion, nausea, low stomach acid, intolerances, dark circles under the eyes, tinnitus, sinus problems, post nasal drip, catarrh, dizziness, fatigue, joint pains, depression (the role of good gut bacteria in mental health is well documented now) and of course digestive problems as mentioned above.

Having antibiotics, medication, alcohol, a lot of sugary foods, smoking and stress can all alter the balance of bacteria in the gut, which can then increase the risk of disease directly or indirectly.

FAST FIXES

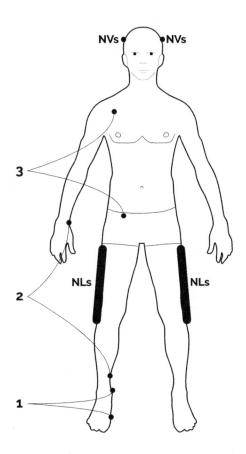

To help get the ICV functioning better, hold the following sets of points in pairs, on the right side of the body, about 30 seconds for each set:

* Along inner edge of foot and inner ankle (1 on the chart)
* 2 inches above inner ankle and on wrist just below the thumb (2 on the chart)
* Halfway along a diagonal line from the navel to hip/ top of thigh and the hollow just below the clavicle (3 on the chart)
* Rub the NLs, shaded areas on chart, massaging along the outer part of the thigh, up and down a few times, please note you are not massaging the skin but the fleshy parts underneath–this can be quite painful
* If you have longer then also hold the NVs on either side of the head above the ears on the ridge for up to a minute

For diarrhoea you can also hold these acu points:

* Touch AP8 on the right side with your right hand
* Touch AP11 on the right side with your left hand
* Hold together for 2- 3 minutes
* Repeat as many times as you like during the day

Or you can use this sequence:

* Touch acu point number 8 on the right side with your right hand
* Touch acu point number 2 on the left side with your left hand
* Hold together for 2- 3 minutes
* Repeat as many times as you like during the day

It is definitely worth looking at your diet, taking a good probiotic and checking out any food intolerances or emotional stresses too.

As I have mentioned at the beginning of the book, I had Ulcerative Colitis when pregnant and it was a combination of various changes to my lifestyle, that all contributed to sorting it out. I found that probiotics, cutting out bread and using kinesiology all really helped. I still take probiotics (because life has its ups and downs), I use these techniques on myself and I now eat bread with no adverse effects.

A word on intolerances. Many people have a test, discover they are intolerant to wheat, dairy etc, give up eating these foods and find that although it makes a difference, it's not always a huge one. This is because there are other factors involved, so helping the body get back into balance using these techniques or seeing a kinesiologist, is part of the process in which the body starts to heal itself so that eventually the body stops reacting adversely to those foods. I have seen many of my clients re introduce foods they were previously intolerant to back into their diet without ill effects. When people have a test but there is no further help to get the body healthy again, they often end up thinking they have to avoid these foods permanently, which is really quite sad.

Please note, I am talking about intolerances not allergies here.

Immune System

Our immune system is very important in keeping us healthy by reacting to external pathogens that invade our bodies and cause infections and illness if we are not able to fight them off.

These invaders can be viruses, bacteria, fungi or parasites.

Once something enters the body and the body detects this as an invader, there are a whole host of responses that are set in motion. Our bodies are very well programmed to fight off these pathogens. The difficulty is when we try to interfere with the process or when our health is poor and the body cannot easily rise to its defence.

Take a cold for instance, as the cold virus works its way into the body, we usually get a sore throat, start sniffling and sneezing, our temperature goes up and we will develop a cough. These are all ways that the body eliminates the toxins produced by the virus and the virus itself. Often, we try to suppress these symptoms, taking cold remedies to reduce the temperature, stop the cough etc. This usually results in the cold lasting over a week with other problems developing as well, sinusitis or maybe a chest infection. A cold should last 3—5 days on average with no resulting health issues.

If our health is compromised then the body finds it much harder to deal with the symptoms and indeed the virus.

A timely example of this is the Corona virus. Young children with healthy immune systems and hopefully less stress have rarely had any problems with this virus.

The people who have had severe problems have been elderly and/or those with pre-existing conditions, so their bodies were already burdened. It was also found that those people with darker skins may have had more difficulty fighting off the virus due to vitamin D deficiency, which has been associated with viral respiratory tract infections and acute lung injury. Vitamin D has been shown to improve the immune response to viral infections. This virus unfortunately is a great example of how different the responses could be, from totally asymptomatic to very sadly in a lot of cases, death.

So, you can see that it is hugely important to keep ourselves as healthy as we can and this will in turn help our immune system to function more efficiently.

A healthy diet with plenty of fruit and vegetables helps our general health as well as our immune system.

Beneficial supplements include vitamin C, vitamin D, zinc and magnesium. Echinacea is a herb that can support the immune system.

NB It can be dangerous for children under the age of 2 to have a high temperature.

FAST FIXES

For a healthy immune system or when you are feeling a bit run down:

* Hold AP3 with AP15 on the same side for 2–3 minutes
* Swap sides and hold for 2–3 minutes

Repeat often when you have a cold, sore throat, fever etc.

*The **Main Central Vertical Energy Flow** is the deepest energy flow in the body and very beneficial for anyone who has chronic illnesses. It is great for helping the back, the spine, the spinal cord and the nervous system, the digestive system, the chakras and the meridian energies. I like to think it re aligns our whole system.*

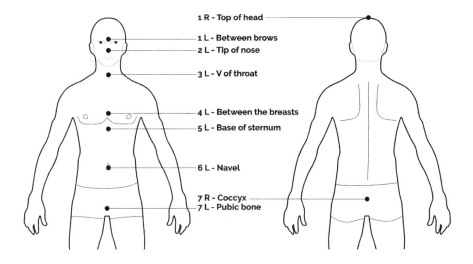

1 R - Top of head
1 L - Between brows
2 L - Tip of nose
3 L - V of throat
4 L - Between the breasts
5 L - Base of sternum
6 L - Navel
7 R - Coccyx
7 L - Pubic bone

* Place your right hand on the top of your head, this remains there until the last step

* Place your left middle finger on the third eye (between the eyebrows) for 2–3 minutes

* Move your left middle finger to the tip of nose, hold for 2–3 minutes

* Move your left middle finger to the "V" of the throat, hold for 2–3 minutes

* Move your left middle finger to the sternum, between the breasts, hold for 2–3 minutes

* Move your left middle finger to the base of sternum (solar plexus) hold for 2–3 minutes

* Move your left middle finger to the navel, hold for 2–3 minutes

* Move your left middle finger to the centre of the pubic bone, hold for 2–3 minutes

* Move your right hand (palm side or back) onto the coccyx, keeping your left hand on the pubic bone. Hold these points for 2–3 minutes

It will probably take you 15–20 minutes, but you can do this whilst reading or watching TV if you like. This is a great flow to use every day as it helps maintain health in spite of the everyday stressors surrounding us and depleting our energy.

This next flow is great for many common ailments such as, sore throats, lung congestion, fever, colds as well as headaches, ear problems and toothache.

* Place your right hand on left side AP12
* Place your left hand on left side AP13
* Hold for 2–3 minutes
* Move your left hand onto left side AP15
* Hold for 2–3 minutes
* Move your left hand onto left side AP1
* Hold for 2–3 minutes
* Swap hands to the other side and repeat

For sinuses and head colds and congestion this works well:

* Hold both of the points AP20s together for 2–3 minutes
* Hold both of the points AP21s together for 2–3 minutes
* Hold both of the points AP22s together for 2–3 minutes

Chronic Fatigue Syndrome (CFS/ME) and Tired all the Time (TATT)

Different syndromes but very similar symptoms and effects. They can have many causes but the effect is that the person affected is always tired, more so than others and never seems to feel the benefit of sleep or rest. In fact, they will often push themselves more because they feel as though they are never doing quite enough.

Rest–as well as sleep–helps, just sitting or lying down quietly doing nothing (no TV, reading etc), this allows the body's energy systems to catch up. A good nutritional supplement containing magnesium will help, as will not expending energy unnecessarily.

Sitting on your hands will help, not to stop you doing anything else, but because your hands will be in contact with the Jin Shin points AP25 (on your sitting bone). Touching these points will help the body regenerate some energy and help relieve mental and physical fatigue. You can also hold AP25 in conjunction with AP11 on the same side to eliminate physical and emotional toxins.

FAST FIXES

* Hold both AP25s for a few minutes, 3 or 4 times a day

When teaching an acupressure workshop, I was talking about the importance of AP25s for energy and one of the ladies who had chronic fatigue said that she would often put her hands on these points and lean against the radiator to keep warm. She was amazed to discover that she had been unconsciously activating these points every day to help her energy levels!

You can also do any or all of these too:

* Hold points AP11 and AP25 on the same side of the body, for a few minutes, then swap hands to the other side and hold for a few minutes, repeat 3 or 4 times a day
* Drink water regularly
* Run the central meridian for a quick energy boost—run your hand up the central line of the body, starting at the pubic bone and stopping just below the bottom lip, take your hand away from the body and repeat twice

You can do a meridian flush which will help any "stuck" energy to disperse and flow as it should around the body. Using the palms of the hands and a light sweeping touch, brush the body with the following movements.

* Run the hands lightly just off the body from the big toes up the inside and front of the legs and up the front of the body to the armpits
* Run each hand in turn from the armpit along the inside of the arm to the finger ends along the palm of the hand. Turn the hand over and run up from the finger tips along back of the hand, arm, shoulder, onto side of head and face, then repeat along the other arm
* Using both hands go from the forehead, over the top and back of head down the back and back of the legs all the way to the feet
* Repeat this sequence 2 more times

This can help clear the daily fatigue:

* Put the fingers of your left hand onto AP19 in the right elbow
* Bend your right arm and place your hand over your right shoulder on AP3
* Hold together for 2–3 minutes
* Repeat on opposite side

Use as often as you like daily.

These next 2 exercises help us if we are affected by adverse EMFs, which people with fatigue issues often are. They help centre us and cope with the effects of gravity, so they can take away the strain of holding ourselves upright. They are also good for back problems.

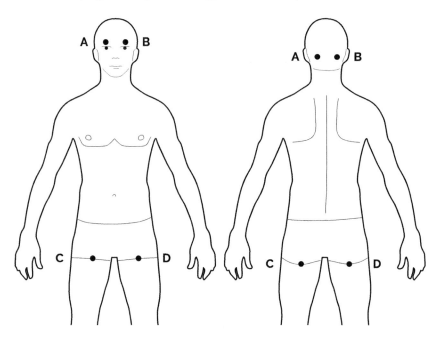

There are 4 pairs of points involved, 2 pairs on the front of the body and 2 pairs on the back. You will be holding one of the head points with one of the lower ones each time.

On the front of the body:

* Touch point A above the eyebrow and contact point C, hold together for up to a minute (A&C)
* Keeping your fingers on A, move the other hand to point D and hold both points for up to a minute (A&D)
* Now move the hand above the eyebrow to the point B and hold with D for up to a minute (B&D)
* Move the lower hand onto C and hold both points for up to a minute (C&D)

This next part uses points on the back of the head, between the back of the ear and the neck and the points on your sitting bone.

* Touch point A on the back of the head and contact point C, hold for up to a minute (A&C)
* Keeping your fingers on A, move the other hand to point D and hold both points for up to a minute (A&D)
* Now move the hand on the back of the head to point B and hold with D for up to a minute (B&D)
* Move the lower hand over to C and hold both points for up to a minute (C&D)

Repeat as needed.

The adrenals are really important when there is fatigue. If they are over-stressed and become exhausted, this can contribute to CFS, digestive problems, lower back problems, allergies, mood swings, headaches and noise sensitivity. Addressing lifestyle factors, diet, cutting out caffeine and other stimulants, will help reduce the stress on the adrenals.

Use this technique to help balance the adrenals:

* Place the fingers of one hand on the back of the head (halfway between the crown and the neck)
* Using the thumb and 2 fingers of the other hand find the points that are 2 inches above and 1 inch to the sides of the navel, push in and rub here firmly for about 10 seconds

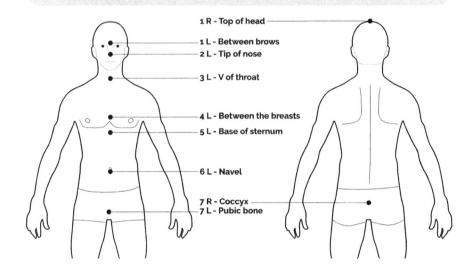

1 R - Top of head
1 L - Between brows
2 L - Tip of nose
3 L - V of throat
4 L - Between the breasts
5 L - Base of sternum
6 L - Navel
7 R - Coccyx
7 L - Pubic bone

The Main Central Vertical Energy Flow is great for helping the back, the spine, spinal cord and nervous system, the digestive system, the chakras and the meridian energies. I like to think it realigns our whole system.

Do this sequence once a day if you can, it will take 15–20 minutes.

* Place your right hand on the top of your head, this remains there until the last step
* Place your left middle finger on the third eye (between the eyebrows) for 2–3 minutes

* Move your left middle finger to the tip of nose, hold for 2–3 minutes

* Move your left middle finger to the "V" of the throat, hold for 2–3 minutes

* Move your left middle finger to the sternum, between the breasts, hold for 2–3 minutes

* Move your left middle finger to the base of sternum (solar plexus) hold for 2–3 minutes

* Move your left middle finger to the navel, hold for 2–3 minutes

* Move your left middle finger to the centre of the pubic bone, hold for 2–3 minutes

* Move your right hand (palm side or back) onto the coccyx, keeping your left hand on the pubic bone. Hold these points for 2–3 minutes

At one High Touch Acupressure class that I taught; the students worked on each other using the Main Central Vertical flow. The next day, one lady said that although she hadn't thought she felt unwell or particularly unhappy before this, she had woken up that morning feeling really well, bright and very positive about the future. So, you can see that this flow can have a very positive effect on us in many different ways.

With ME, CFS or TATT the main thing to remember here, is to do self-help little and often. As the energy reserves here are so low and need building up, it is helpful to remember that any treatment, whether it is complementary or conventional, requires energy from the body to process and actuate it. Medication requires energy to be metabolised. Energy work also requires the body's own energy to process and utilise what's put into it. If the treatment in a relatively healthy person uses 10% of their energy reserves, the person has enough left for the body's normal functions. In someone who has health issues and their energy reserves are very depleted, that same amount of energy in a healthy person could be equivalent to say 50% of the energy reserves in someone who's unwell. This means that they can become very depleted in energy, before the body can produce more from the beneficial effects of the treatment. It is better to do small amounts, more often, which will use less energy initially and build up slowly. Better to do a few minutes 2 or 3 times a day, rather than once a day for 30 minutes.

The Liver

It has been said that if you treat the liver, it will help 85% of illnesses!

If you suffer from headaches, migraines, PMS, hot flushes, IBS, flatulence or constipation and even skin problems, this could be a sign of liver overload and poor detoxification.

The liver has well over 400 known functions in the body; as well as distributing nutrients around the body, it plays a key role in most metabolic processes, especially detoxification. It neutralises a wide range of toxins and helps dispose of unwanted hormones to name but a few of its functions.

Given our culture today of many more unhealthy foods, the body has to work so much harder to dispose of the unwanted by products from these (in part contributing to the food intolerances that may develop when the body is under stress). Environmental toxins have increased over the years, the air, our water, chemicals sprayed onto fruit and veg, hormones and antibiotics in meat, all add up to a toxic overload for the liver to dispose of.

There are 2 phases to liver detoxification, the first involves the liver filtering out impurities in the blood. Blood from the intestines contains high levels of toxic material, so having the liver fully functioning means that these are removed before they can affect other organs.

The second phase involves bile and fibre in the gut which helps absorb the toxins and allows them to be flushed out. This is one of the reasons why a high fibre diet is important.

Toxins remaining in the body interfere with its metabolism–remember what a hangover feels like? A healthy liver and healthy gut are both necessary to keep the body healthy.

To help keep your liver in top form, eat plenty of fruit and vegetables especially brassicas (broccoli, cauliflower, kale etc) and wholegrain foods.

Supplements that will also help include probiotics and milk thistle is one of the herbs that support the liver. Vitamin C and the B vitamins, magnesium and zinc are all involved in the metabolic pathways for detoxification.

FAST FIXES

To help with liver detox:

* Place your hands over the points AP14s and hold for 2–3 minutes (can be done with crossed hands if easier)
* Keep one hand on the right side AP14 and move the other hand on to the left side AP11
* Hold together for 2–3 minutes
* Now swap sides
* Hold together for 2–3 minutes

More help for the liver:

* Hold left AP4 and right AP14 together for 2–3 minutes
* Hold right AP4 and left AP14 together for 2–3 minutes

Repeat both as needed.

You can also rub the Lv NLs to stimulate the lymphatic reflexes of the liver to help it process any burden and aid detoxification. Plenty of water also helps too.

* Rub the Lv NLs firmly along the right rib area where a bra wire would be, for about 30 seconds

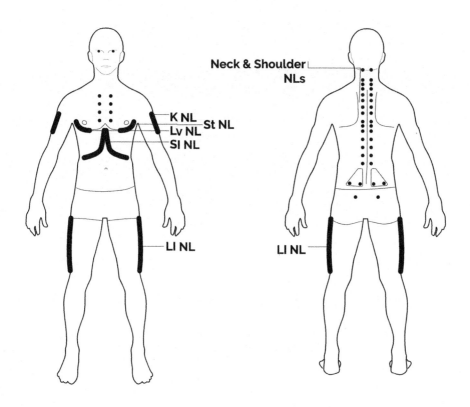

PMS

Pre-Menstrual Syndrome can be very debilitating for some women from early teens to early fifties, one week out of four. When added up this could be up to 456 weeks, equating to nearly 9 years of a woman's life!

Symptoms range from breast pain, feeling bloated, mood swings, irritability, depression, anxiety, clumsiness, stomach cramps, feeling sick, food cravings, headaches, weight gain, to difficulty sleeping and lack of concentration. It usually eases when menstruation starts, although for many women there can be pain and cramps during their period too.

The liver can be involved with PMS. During that time before a period the liver has a role to play in processing the hormones so that they can be excreted from the body more easily. If the liver is congested, then the hormones fail to be eliminated properly and this causes hormonal imbalance.

Unsurprisingly, the emotions that are related to PMS are the same as those related to liver meridian energy imbalance.

FAST FIXES

To help balance up the hormones, linking the reflex points on the hands for the pituitary and ovaries can help.

* Place your right middle finger over the whorl at the centre of your left thumb
* Place your right thumb on the outer edge of the hand below the little finger just above the wrist crease (AP17)
* Hold together for 2–3 minutes
* Swap hands and repeat

To help with bloating and swelling in the abdomen and pelvic areas:

* Place one hand on AP1
* Place the other hand on AP2 on the opposite side
* Hold them together for a few minutes and then swap sides

Repeat as often as you like during the day.

To help with detoxification:

* Hold AP11 with the opposite side AP13 for a few minutes
* Swap sides and repeat
* Hold both high 19s together for a couple of minutes

High 19s are above AP19, midway between the elbow crease and the shoulder.

These points can help the hormonal balance:

* Place one hand on point AP13
* Place the other hand on the same side AP8
* Hold together for 2–3 minutes
* Swap hands and repeat

To help with the emotional effects of PMS

* Place your fingers on AP14
* Place your other hand over AP19 on the same side

This can be a bit awkward to do, so just adapt the positions of your hands and fingers to make it work in the best way for you.

For menstrual pain:

* Tap the points Sp 2 (see page 56)
* About 30 taps at a beat of 1 tap per second
* Reassess pain and if it is still there, tap again, 30 taps
* Stop when either the pain has gone or it is reduced and further tapping doesn't seem to change it anymore

I shared this with a client who was having very painful periods. She told me that when the pains started and she did the tapping, at first nothing happened, but then 3 minutes later the pain stopped. She continued to tap occasionally for the next few days and she said that although she could tell there was still some cramping, the pain just wasn't there anymore.

More help with menstrual pain and nausea:

* Put your fingers on the point low 8 (found a hands width below AP8 on the side of the leg)
* Put the fingers of the other hand onto AP16 on the same leg
* Hold points for 2–3 minutes
* Swap hands and repeat

For breast tenderness, cysts:

* Place fingers on painful area
* With the other hand firmly rub the outside of the thighs from hipbone to knee in a downward direction 6 or 7 times (LI NLs)

This is also good to use for lumps, cysts or spots anywhere on body.

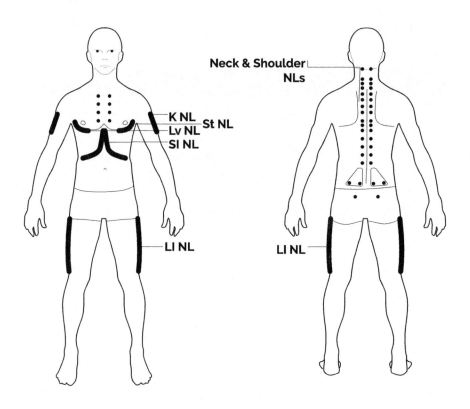

Hot flushes

There are many factors to do with the menopause which can cause problems such as hot flushes, fatigue, sleep problems, weight gain and more.

Hot flushes occur around the time of the menopause and sometimes for much longer afterwards. They can last for 30 seconds to several minutes and can be very uncomfortable to endure.

When oestrogen levels fall, the adrenal glands take over, producing small amounts of oestrogen. If the adrenals are constantly stressed— tea, coffee, cigarettes and sugar can all do this, then they are not able to deliver the oestrogen required to keep the hormonal balance. The body may respond to that stressor by flushing.

A good starting point would be to cut out caffeine, cigarettes, sugary foods and drinks. Sometimes even just a hot drink can tip the balance in the body's heat processing and bring on a hot flush.

Taking Vitamin C and a multi B vitamin supplement can both help to support the adrenals.

If the liver is sluggish then this can affect how the body processes toxins, and can result in fatigue, rashes, irritable bowel, bloating and gaining weight too.

There are also quite a few herbs that can help with the adrenals, hormones, and the liver. When oestrogen levels fall, phytoestrogens can help. These include soya, red clover and other herbs which have a balancing effect on the hormones.

The trick is knowing which of those factors the body wants help with as a priority and this is where kinesiology comes into its own. It can determine which factors are contributing to the problems and also the right herbs, supplements and kinesiology corrections to get the body back into balance again.

FAST FIXES

This works on the reflex area for the pituitary gland and can have a positive effect on temperature control.

* Press in the centre of the fingerprint whorl of each thumb for about 10 seconds
* Repeat as needed

You can follow this up by linking the reflex points on the hands for the pituitary and ovaries:

* Place your right middle finger over the whorl at the centre of your left thumb
* Place your right thumb on the outer edge of the hand below the little finger just above the wrist crease (AP17)
* Hold together for 2–3 minutes
* Swap hands and repeat

This is great for hot flushes:

* Place one hand on point AP13
* Place the other hand on the same side AP8
* Hold together for 2–3 minutes
* Swap hands and repeat

More help for hormonal balance and hot flushes:

* Place fingers of one hand on AP13
* Place the other hand over the shoulder, contacting the AP11

* Hold together for 2–3 minutes
* Swap hands and repeat
* Move both hands to high 19s for 2–3 minutes

High 19s are above AP19, midway between the elbow crease and the shoulder.

Sedating the TW meridian can help the hormonal balance, as well as helping with stress.

* Starting from the outer edge of the eyebrows
* Move your fingers around the back of the ear, down the neck and the arms as far as is comfortable
* Repeat 3 or 4 times on both sides

Your fingers can either touch the skin or can be an inch or so from the body when you do this.

The Skin

The skin is actually the largest organ in the body. It covers our muscles, connective tissue and internal organs. It is waterproof (to a degree) and as it has hair follicles, it provides us with a warm covering of hair.

Our skin reflects what is going on in our body and also what is happening in our life. When we are irritated, our skin can become irritated and inflamed too. If our digestion isn't brilliant, neither is the skin, it can look pasty and doughy reflecting the inflammation that is going on inside. When we are physically tired, our skin looks tired too.

Itchy irritated skin, rashes and dermatitis may be due to food or chemical intolerances and kinesiology can help detect these. Helping the liver is often of great benefit too for the skin.

Dry skin reflects that the body is dehydrated and you need to drink more water. It can also indicate that the mineral balance is wrong, so a good multi mineral supplement may help too. However, dehydration can be due to many other causes. For instance, constipation and diarrhoea or liver overload from food, alcohol or from processing too many toxins.

These days with the obsession about looking good, it is often not enough to cleanse our skin, have the odd facial and put make up on to cover the worst. We need to address the internal disorders that affect our skin externally.

Hormonal disruptions and emotional issues reflect in eruptions on the skin, on the face, the back of the neck and also the back. For hormonally related skin issues, teenage acne, blemishes pre-menstruation, during pregnancy and around the menopause, zinc can often help as this is used up in great quantities to produce hormones. Zinc is especially helpful for teenage boys when their hormones are changing.

NB Zinc should not be taken during the last 2 months in pregnancy.

Probiotics (good bacteria) have a very beneficial effect on the skin, as they help the gut become healthy and happy. What affects our internal skin (the gut) is reflected in our external skin too. Indeed, many skin products now have probiotics in their ingredients.

Research[12] has shown that over 50% of the DNA in our bodies is actually bacterial, much of it concentrated in the gut. We really want those bacteria to be beneficial for us.

Dysbiosis (imbalance in the bacteria colonies) creates toxicity in the gut which puts a strain on our bodies to remove it and has a knock-on effect in other areas, including the liver and the skin.

Skin brushing the body has a beneficial and twofold effect on the skin.

Firstly, by dislodging dry dead cells and debris from the surface of the skin, the stimulation from brushing brings blood to the surface, giving the skin a brighter healthier glow.

Secondly, it stimulates the tissues under the surface of the skin which has the effect of moving toxins in the connective tissue and the interstitial fluid into the lymph which eventually drains into the blood vessels. When this reaches the liver, it is reprocessed and dispersed into the bowel for elimination out of the body.

If you go for a whole-body massage this too helps the skin, blood circulation and lymph flow, again draining toxins away and having a beneficial effect on all areas of the body.

Facials and facial massage, facial reflexology all have a rejuvenating and therapeutic effect on the appearance of the facial skin.

FAST FIXES

Skin brushing, although this should actually be called skin stroking as the intention is to very gently brush the skin to stimulate the movement of the lymph fluid just under the skin. This should be done using a good quality bristle brush.

* Use long strokes to brush the body using upward movements on all sides of the legs and trunk of the body towards the upper chest
* The arms should be brushed from finger tips to the armpits (all sides), again towards the upper part of the chest, which is where the lymph fluid enters the bloodstream
* Remember to do the neck and décolletage area in a downward movement here

Sorting out the cause of digestive problems can have a resulting beneficial effect on the skin too. Hence some of the techniques described elsewhere for the issues mentioned above will all have a knock-on effect in benefitting the skin indirectly. Especially working on the Ileo Caecal Valve (ICV) which can help so many problems that are seemingly not connected.

To help get the ICV functioning better, hold the following sets of points in pairs on the right side of the body only, for about 30 seconds on each set.

* Both 1s along inner edge of foot and inner ankle (1 on chart)
* Both 2s 2 inches above inner ankle and on wrist just below the thumb (2 on chart)
* Halfway along a diagonal line from the navel to hip/top of thigh and the hollow just below the clavicle (3 on chart)
* Rub the NLs downwards and upwards a few times, massaging along the outer part of the thigh, please note you are not massaging the skin but the fleshy parts underneath–this can be quite painful
* If you have longer then you can also hold the NVs on either side of the head above the ears on the ridge for up to a minute

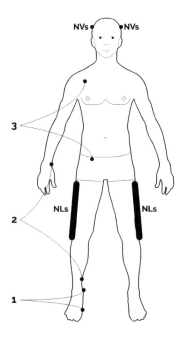

To help generally with detoxification:

* Hold AP11 with the opposite side AP13 for a few minutes
* Swap sides and repeat
* Hold both high 19s together for a couple of minutes

High 19s are above points AP19, midway between the elbow crease and the shoulder

To help with liver detox:

* Place your hands over the points AP14s and hold for 2–3 minutes (this can be done with crossed hands if easier)

You can also do this one too:

* Keep your hand on the right side AP14 and move your other hand on to the left side AP11
* Hold together for 2–3 minutes
* Now swap sides
* Hold together for 2–3 minutes

For the face, facial reflex and acupressure points that will help:

* Using the middle fingers press gently, starting at the inner corner of the eyebrows and moving slowly along the bony parts of the eye sockets around the eye, until you reach the start point
* Press both of the points at the inner corner of the eyebrows for 5–10 seconds
* Press both of the points next to the nose, halfway down the nose for 5–10 seconds
* Press both of the points next to the nose, at the bottom of the nose for 5–10 seconds
* Do all of this sequence three times

More acupressure points for the face:

* Hold both points AP20 for 2–3 minutes
* Hold both points AP21 for 2–3 minutes
* Hold both points AP22 for 2–3 minutes

Cellulite

There are many remedies available for use externally on the skin. However, the best ways to help reduce cellulite is by eliminating toxins from the body, relieving stress and by weight loss. These actions will all help the tissue to release its stored toxins. The body can't do this if it is already overloaded (in other words if we are stressed, tired, under the weather or ill), as it is already processing as much as it can handle. Any excess is stored in fat cells, as cellulite or beer belly and joints.

Kinesiology clients would find that as well as their presenting problems being resolved, they would feel less bloated and often as an added bonus their cellulite would disappear too.

Generally, cellulite dispersal will be helped by eliminating sugary and processed foods, as well as choosing healthy and invigorating foods and better lifestyle choices.

FAST FIXES

* Let your arms relax down by your sides
* In the area where your fingertips touch the side of your thighs is a sore spot (you may have to move your fingers up or down slightly, but you'll know when you've found it)
* Massage this point quite firmly

This can be very sore, it is known as the toxic point, for obvious reasons.

* Hold high 1s with opposite hands and with your fingers pointing downwards for a few minutes
* Do this frequently and daily

High 1s are found a hand span up the thigh from AP1s.

To help with detoxification:

* Massage firmly the cellulite area on the thighs whilst holding the opposite side AP11
* Swap to the other leg and repeat

Restless legs

This syndrome tends to affect women more than men and more so around the time of the menopause. For a lot of people there is no obvious cause, however for some there may be an underlying health condition. Exercise is known to help and also cutting down on caffeine and drinking more water.

FAST FIXES

To help with detoxification:

* Place your hands over the points AP14s and hold for 2–3 minutes (can be done with crossed hands if easier)
* Keep hand on the right side AP14 and move your other hand on to the left side AP11
* Hold together for 2–3 minutes
* Now swap sides
* Hold together for 2–3 minutes

These points can help the hormonal balance:

* Place fingers on both points AP8 and hold together for 2–3 minutes
* Place fingers on both points AP13 and hold together for 2–3 minutes
* Place fingers on both points AP6 and hold together for 2–3 minutes

The acupressure points AP1 and AP2 are really helpful for leg problems.

* Place one hand on AP1
* Place the other hand on AP2 on the same side
* Hold them together for a few minutes and then swap sides

Or you can use the same points in a slightly different way, go with which feels the best for you:

* Place one hand on AP1
* Place the other hand on AP2 on the opposite side
* Hold them together for a few minutes and then swap sides

Repeat as often as you like during the day.

When you are in bed and your legs become restless, you can use a point on the hands which will help calm things down. This point relates to the Triple Warmer meridian which is most active between 9–11pm. This is probably around the time you are drifting off to sleep and this is when restless legs often occur. You could also do this before going to bed.

* Tap the point on the back of the hand TW 3, 30 times (see page 56)
* Swap hands and repeat

Repeat the tapping 2 or 3 times for maximum benefit.

Bunions and bony lumps on feet

It's amazing how the feet can end up with all sorts of lumps and bumps on them, they take a lot of wear and tear from walking, standing and from shoes. If we have knee, back or hip problems then these can affect the way we position our feet when walking. If there is long term stress on some of the joints there can be inflammation and distortion which can produce bony growths.

The most common of these is the bunion on the joint at the base of the big toe. As you will know if you have one, they can be very painful.

One thing I have often recommended to clients is to use toe separators (the ones you use when painting your toenails) for about 20 minutes a day. I've found this really helps to stop further distortion and can even help ease the toes back into alignment, a bit like wearing a brace on the teeth.

FAST FIXES

> * Place the north pole side of a magnet on the painful area for about 20 minutes, once a week or so

One of my clients had a bony lump that was growing slowly and because it was at the top of her foot it was starting to cause a problem with wearing some of her shoes. Every time she came for reflexology, I popped a magnet over this part of her foot and the lump slowly started to shrink. This also works on scars that give discomfort.

For bunions:

> * Massage all around the base of the thumb on the same side of body as the bunion (or both if bunions on both feet), especially at the outer edge

Look at the thumb in relation to the big toe and you can see that the second joint on the outer edge relates to the bunion.

Cystitis

This presents as a burning sensation or pain when urinating. Cystitis can be due to a urinary tract or kidney infection. It can also be from irritation of the urinary tract, maybe from too much caffeine, not enough water, or too much protein in the diet. The urine may be a darker colour and smelly too.

The supplement D-Mannose can help with recurrent infections and it's worth checking if you are drinking enough water.

FAST FIXES

If it's more bladder related:

* Place fingers on AP2
* Place other hand on the opposite side AP15
* Hold together for 2–3 minutes
* Move hand from AP15 to AP1, again on the opposite side to other hand
* Hold together for 2–3 minutes
* Move hand from 1 to AP8, again on the opposite side to other hand
* Hold together for 2–3 minutes
* Swap sides and repeat

For cystitis in general:

* Hold both points AP8s for 2–3 minutes
* Move hands to the low 8s (1 hands width from AP8 down the side of the calf)
* Hold these points together for 2–3 minutes

* Move hands to AP16s
* Hold these points together for 2–3 minutes
* Move hands to AP24s
* Hold these points together for 2–3 minutes
* Move hands to the little toes
* Hold them together for 2–3 minutes

You can do these a few times during the day.

Quite often after a bout of cystitis, there can be a sensation of wanting to pass water more often than normal, when the bladder isn't actually full. This can also happen for many women, for what appears to be no reason. This technique helps to reset the nerves to the bladder to stop that sensation of "wanting to go" when it's not really necessary.

You will need to get someone to do this for you.

* Lay on the floor with your knees bent and the soles of the feet on the floor
* Make sure your knees are together
* Ask the person to use firm pressure to attempt to push your knees apart a few times, while you resist the movement

Quite a few of my clients find this invaluable. It relieves that sensation of fullness and frequently having the urge to pass water, but when you go there is hardly anything there.

Hering's Law of Cure

I have mentioned the energy of the acupressure points and how by connecting those points, this can help the energy to flow more effectively around the body. We also have energy surrounding us, the aura contains the blueprint of our physical body.

When our aura is affected this can lead to physical changes in the body.

There are more and more external electromagnetic fields around us which could be damaging if we don't look after ourselves and nurture ourselves with healthy lifestyle choices.

Many years ago, when I had just started learning kinesiology, I was introduced to the test vials that a lot of kinesiologists use. I had my new kit and was practising on my friends. One friend was very fit and healthy with an extremely healthy diet and she exercised every day either walking or going to the gym. I'd tested her a couple of times with my new kit and nothing was amiss, until the next time when the vial for osteoporosis showed up. I was shocked, she was the last person I would have expected to be susceptible to this. I asked her if anything had changed, her reply was that she hadn't had time to do her usual walking and exercise over the last 10 days. I found this amazing, she didn't actually have osteoporosis but the test vials had shown the energy associated with this had changed. I took this to mean that if she carried on with not exercising for a good length of time then this could eventually lead to osteoporosis.

Emotional thoughts and processes affect us too, altering hormones and chemicals within the body. These are normal changes, tears eliminate toxins, anger outbursts utilise adrenalin, but if prolonged, then they can bring about permanent changes.

A change in emotional equilibrium changes the messages sent by the neurotransmitters to cells in the relevant parts of the body. Dr Christine

Page in her book Frontiers of Health, says that if those new signals are maintained for more than 5 days, then there can be permanent neurological changes. So, it appears that disease starts externally and moves inwards as it progresses.

Constantine Hering was a German who became very influential in the field of homeopathy in the 1800s. His observations of how a person heals from disease became known as Hering's Law of Cure.

The Law of Cure allows you to understand the process of healing when using complementary therapies/medicine. Conventional medicine tends to suppress or mask the symptoms of an illness to help us feel better. However, symptoms are a result of the body trying to do something to expel the problem. If we eat something that may be "off", the digestive system reacts quite quickly to rid itself of the substance. If it didn't, then the toxin (whether it's a bacteria or noxious chemical produced from the food being off) could linger in the body. Similarly, with a cold we sneeze, cough and have a runny nose, as the body reacts to the invasive virus.

If these symptoms are suppressed, the virus, bacteria or toxic substance can stay in the body and wreak much more havoc.

When we are dealing with longer term conditions, for instance chronic sinusitis, the body may get a fever to help burn off the toxins, which will then be eliminated from the body in various ways. If it's via the lungs, then it will be accompanied by lots of mucous (phlegm). If the bowels are affected there may again be much mucous and possibly old, stuck faeces. Elimination can also take place through the skin, causing a breakout of spots, eczema or irritation.

Hering noticed that as the body starts to heal, internal symptoms and organs of the body start to clear first and the external symptoms and the skin, which is an external organ, follows later.

I too have seen this with clients. Those who have asthma, hay fever or suffer a lot from chest infections will often get eczema, dry skin or some sort of skin irritation as their other symptoms disappear. If a person with eczema can see their skin getting better but then they start to have asthma or hay fever this is a sign that the condition has actually worsened. I had a client whose asthma went but the eczema she had suffered from as a child came back quite badly. Although this appeared to be a setback, it was actually a sign that her body was healing. And eventually the eczema disappeared too.

Hering also observed that the body will heal in reverse order to how the symptoms appeared, meaning that a person's symptoms will appear and disappear in the reverse order of their appearance upon the body. This can be seen with children for instance who have eczema when very young that clears as they get older but they go on to develop asthma or hay fever. When their bodies start to heal from the hay fever or asthma, they will often get a resurgence of the original skin condition.

One of my first reflexology clients was an elderly gentleman who after his third session had a brief recurrence of varicose eczema, a condition he had a lot when he was much younger, fortunately this time it only lasted three days!

Many years ago, I was lucky enough to be taught Clinical Medicine and Alternative Clinical Medicine by Dr. Rodney Adeniyi-Jones, a very well-respected kinesiologist as well as a medical doctor. He gave an example of a patient who had had liver cancer and was well on the road to recovery when he had a recurrence of hepatitis. Rodney remarked, "It wasn't a big problem on the way in, so it won't be on the way out!"

Another of Hering's observations was that symptoms may clear from the head and top of the body first. I have seen this myself, time and time again with clients telling me that "they just feel better in themselves". They feel uplifted after a treatment, calmer, more relaxed, their head and mind feel clearer and lighter. There may also be an emotional release, tears or anger for instance. Another example is, neck problems that clear up before lower back problems.

Take someone with IBS and knee problems, as they start to heal, their digestive system will start to function better but their knees may not feel much different at first. This can arise because the digestive system as well as taking in nutrients, plays an important part in the proper elimination of toxins. If it's not fulfilling these functions, toxins may get deposited in the joints or fat cells. It makes sense that getting the digestive system fully functioning and eliminating efficiently, enables toxins to clear better. So now those that have been "stored" in the joints and fat cells can be removed and eliminated. Resulting in weight loss and less painful joints.

Hering's Law states that the body will heal:

* From above moving downwards
* From within moving outwards
* From a more important organ to a less important one
* In the reverse order of disease

As you use this book, you can refer to Hering's Law of Cure if you would like to know how well your body is progressing along the journey of health improvement and why there may be the odd detour.

Preventative Health

As mentioned previously, complementary therapies were originally intended to be preventative. I find that clients will often carry on having regular sessions long after their original problem has cleared up. They recognise that because lifestyle factors continue to impact on them, regular sessions help to keep them in good health.

Just as we eat healthily and exercise regularly and we know we feel better for doing this, now there is evidence to show that it can prevent conditions such as osteoporosis, diabetes, heart and circulatory problems. Use the techniques from this book that you have found have improved your health, to help you stay healthy and prevent dis-ease. Here are some other ideas to help you maintain good health and wellbeing.

Injury recall

Whenever you have something happen that causes some sort of new trauma to the body (a twisted ankle, stubbed toe, pulled muscle, a bruised head from a cupboard door, a mammogram, a filling in a tooth, etc) use this technique. You only need to do it once per injury.

It is probably easier to ask someone else to do this for you:

* Put your hand over the injury site
* The other person holds your heel still with one hand and then grasps the top of your foot at the ankle end and pushes it down (towards the sole of the foot) firmly on the same side as the injury (if relevant) 3 or 4 times
* Repeat on the other foot, 3 or 4 times

This actually not only helps further healing of the trauma; it has been demonstrated to increase the flexibility of the joints and allow further movement of the hips and shoulders.

Emotional Stress Release (ESR) for pain

At the time of the physical injury or trauma there is always an emotional component involved.

This is an excellent technique to use whenever you can after you experience a physical injury. You can also use it if long standing pain is emotionally draining.

There are points on the forehead that help release the emotional stress attached to a situation and also balance hormone levels in relation to that situation. These points are excellent for any stress, not just pain.

* Place one hand on the painful area
* Put your thumb and two fingers of the other hand onto the points on the forehead AP20s
* Think about where the pain is located
* Think about the quality of the pain, what it feels like when it hurts, whether it is a sharp pain, achy or sore, think about if it is constant or just there some of the time and also when it occurs
* Think about what actually happened to cause the pain. Where you were and what you were doing when it happened, i.e. the memory associated with the pain
* Then after a few minutes you can change those thoughts, feeling calmer and visualising how you would feel, and be, without the pain affecting you

I've found so many times with clients that just using these two techniques at the beginning of a session has drastically decreased the person's pain levels. They also help the body's healing process.

This exercise helps all the cranial nerves and especially the vagus nerve. These nerves contribute to calming the body's autonomic nervous system, releasing anxiety. This is something you can do every day if you like and especially before using other techniques. It is said to increase the beneficial effect of other techniques.

* Interlink the fingers of both hands and put your hands behind your head, covering the base of the skull and the hollows beneath this
* Then keeping the head still, move your eyes to the right, until you take a deep breath or feel a sigh coming on
* Bring your eyes back to the centre
* Repeat the eye movement to the other side

If you don't notice a sigh or a deep breath, just keep the eyes in position for about a minute, on each side.

I have mentioned this previously, it really is a good all-rounder to do at any time.

* Rubbing your ears, all over inside and out, front and back, stimulates the mini acupuncture system reflected on the ear

It acts almost like a mini massage for the body, as well as stimulating the blood flow to the brain helping us feel more alert.

This is great for helping to increase our general body range of motion.

* Tap firmly with the fingertips all over the front, back and sides of the ribcage

High Touch Acupressure (Jin Shin) APs 1–26

Please see section on 'How to use the fixes', for introductory information about these acupressure points.

The 26 Points can be used in many different ways, either individually i.e. both points together or with their partner point as shown in the chart at the end of the point descriptions.

Each point has its own meaning and purpose as described below. You can look through these and find the points or flow that is beneficial for you at this particular time and use that combination of points.

They help physically, mentally, emotionally and spiritually.

It's amazing how our body can hold on to memories that our conscious mind has forgotten, or events we thought we had already dealt with. Jin Shin releases blocked energy in layers, rather like peeling an onion. We can't get to the bottom of the layer until the top layers are cleared. We all react differently when layers are cleared out, and self-care is important after any energy session.

You just need to lightly touch these points with your fingers and hold for 2–3 minutes, or longer if you have time. As you become more aware of what is happening in your body you may find that you will feel, or know when the point has cleared and you are ready to move on.

You can also feel pulses in your fingers as you work more with these points, in which case when the pulses synchronise, the blockage has cleared. You can then hold for a bit longer before releasing. If you don't feel these pulses, then just hold for 2–3 minutes. If the area is painful to touch or you can't quite reach then you can hold them an inch or so off the body, you will still be contacting them energetically.

You can be quite creative with these points too.

For instance, if you have a knee problem you would definitely want to include the AP1 points, as these are for moving forward. The first thing we do when wanting to take a step, is to bend the knee.

You could combine the AP1 point on the affected knee with the point AP26 on the opposite side to clear the congestion.

You could hold both AP1 and AP8 together on the problematic knee.

If you are also having problems with the hip, back or pelvic area as well as the knee, you can hold the points AP1 and AP2 together. If it's the same side hip and knee then hold the points AP1 and AP2 on the same side, if it's opposite sides then hold the points on the opposite sides too.

If you can't decide or if both knees are affected, you can just hold both AP1s.

When using these acupressure points, depending on what the problem is, then:

* If the problem, pain or inflammation is on right side—treat the right side

* If the problem, pain or inflammation is on left side—treat the left side

* If the problem is in the present, if you are aware of what may be causing it, or if a male energy is involved, then treat the right side

* If the problem is from the past, if you don't know why it has happened, or if a female energy is involved, then treat the left side

* Use your intuition, whichever side you instinctively choose

* If in doubt do the right side first to clear the present, then the left to clear the past

The 26 High Touch Acupressure Points (APs)

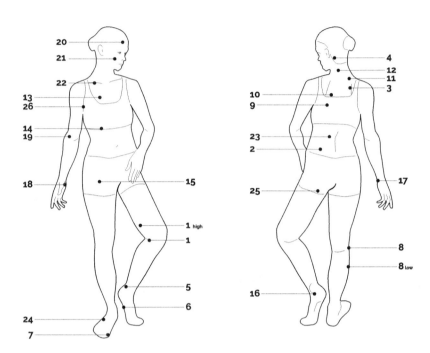

When using these points, hold the combinations together for 2–3 minutes on each set.

AP1 The Prime Mover

This first point, number 1, is to help support us with change and to be open minded in new ventures and taking steps forward in life. New job, college, new relationship, maybe moving on emotionally, as well as opening up and developing our spiritual side. Helping us with life changes, it helps us move forward when we are stuck.

Fittingly it is located on the inside of the knee, the part we move first when physically taking a step forward. Hence it is known as the Prime Mover.

This point will help put the past behind you and step into the unknown.

It also rejuvenates all the other 26 points, so if in doubt as to which points to use, hold 1 and the opposite side 26 together. This combination helps us move forward and clear out anything from the past that would hinder us from taking that new step in life.

The left knee, relates to the past, unconscious, emotional, feminine side of us.

The right knee relates to the present, what we are conscious of, the masculine side.

Physically, the AP1 points can help with arthritis, sore knees, and cold feet, abdominal bloating and headaches too.

> * Hold both 1s together
> * Or hold 1 with 26 on the opposite side

There is also a related point, the high 1, find it by placing your fingers on AP1 lightly stretch your fingers out up the inside of the thigh and where thumb rests, is high 1.

Good for digestive problems, stomach pain, bloating and difficulty in sleeping after a heavy meal.

> * For high 1s, hold both together

AP2 Wisdom

This is on top of the hipbone about 5cm either side of the spine, (find the soft spot and hold it gently and either wait for pulses, or hold for 2–3 minutes).

This point helps the creative life force within us, it brings bright ideas as well as wisdom. It's important for our self-survival, as it helps with our Jing energy, the deep energy reserves that we are born with–determines the quality and quantity of our vitality.

If there is congestion within these points, it can make us apathetic, not interested in life.

Physically it's said to be good for the reproductive organs, kidney, prostate problems, hip and back problems.

* Hold both 2s together
* Or hold 2 and same side 3 together
* Or hold 2 and 1 together to keep the energy moving when taking that step forwards

AP3 The Door

This is the door between the head and the heart, intellect and feeling. It brings understanding and the ability to express feelings.

Situated on top of the scapula either side of the spine, it acts as a defence mechanism against outside forces that could be destructive, energetically and emotionally as well as physically.

AP3s can be blocked when someone is feeling emotional and finding it hard to be objective, or conversely when someone intellectualises their feelings.

Physically it can help our breathing, speech and shoulders. It helps stimulate the immune system by "shutting the door" to germs. We can also use it for colds, fevers, sore throats, anything immune related. If you are struggling to feel awake in the morning, try holding these points to start your day.

* Either hold both 3s together
* Or hold 3 with the same side 15 to let joy into your life

AP4 The Window

This point is at the occipital area at the base of the head, either side of the spine. It is known as The Window, because this is where the life force is said to enter. It is also known as the Intellectual Collector helping to take information into the brain. These points help us assimilate information, so they are great for when studying and analysing information.

The AP4 points help when we are overthinking and when there is constant mind chatter. They help to bring order, mentally.

These points are excellent for insomnia, so you can hold AP4s either at bedtime, to get off to sleep or if you are prone to waking up with your mind becoming overactive, use these points then.

Because of their connection with the brain and information they are said to help with Parkinsons, Alzheimers and memory. They can also help with a sore throat.

> * Hold both 4s together for sleep issues
> * Or hold 4 with opposite side 21, then swap sides

AP5 Freedom from Fear

This point is located on the inside of the ankle. It's associated with fear and when we are contemplating big moves of any kind, fear, apprehension and anxiety often accompany this. Fear freezes us, it stops us from moving forward in life.

The ankle is the second part of the body to move when taking a step, so clearing AP5 will help us get unstuck and move beyond fear to experience life.

Physically these points help with the ankles, hips and kidneys.

> * 5 and 1 together are an excellent combination to liberate us from fear so we can move forward with confidence and positive expectation
> * Or hold 5 and same side 16 to help let go of the past

AP6 Balance

Found on the inside arch of the foot, this point has a balancing effect. The arch of the foot helps us maintain our balance and stand on our own two feet; it can keep us grounded. If there is anger or grief either from the past or in the present, this can block AP6, so holding both of these points together can balance the emotions.

Physically it can help with the feet, cold feet, cramps and the opposite hip.

* When there is disorder and chaos in your life hold 24 and 6 together, on both feet
* Or hold 6 with same side 15
* Or hold 6 with same side 3

AP7 Victory

Situated on the big toe, this point signifies victory and completion of what you have undertaken. It brings peace, security and abundance.

Physically it's good for alleviating headaches and clearing the mind.

* Hold 7 and opposite 12 together

AP8 The Magician

This is behind the knees on the outside edge. It brings illumination, helping us see the light so that we can make sense of things. It can help us let go of old belief systems so we can be open to the new. It helps us be in the flow of life—rather than against it.

It is also the "hormone specialist", use it for PMT, menopause and the prostate. It helps with the pelvic area and also elimination. It rules the magic of reproduction and rejuvenation, it is said to keep you young!

* Hold 8 and same 11 together

Low 8 is about a hand span below AP8, this can be used for muscle problems, leg cramps and twitching eyes. It is also said to help with skeletal problems.

* Hold both low 8s together

AP9 Transitions

On the bottom tip of scapula, this helps us with changes and transitions, endings and beginnings, helping us to let go of old stuff and welcome the new.

As it is difficult to reach on yourself, you can substitute it with AP19 which is in the crease of the elbow, to release AP9. Anger and grief can get stuck in AP9s, holding these points helps collect and release past stuff so that we don't take it with us going forward.

Physically these points are said to help with arthritis, breathing, asthma, the upper back and neck.

* Hold both 19s
* Or hold 19 and opposite 1 together for bloating

AP10 Compassionate Love

These points are halfway up the shoulder blade on the spine side. On yourself use high 19s which are found halfway up the arm from AP19.

They are often blocked by self-blame, guilt, hate and judgement of ourselves and others. A blocked AP10 is often present in people who care for others to the detriment of themselves. An open AP10 is for limitless power, strength and forgiveness of ourselves and others, letting go of the past, releasing pain, regret and resentment, so we can regain peace in the present. Compassion helps us forgive ourselves and others so we can be receptive to love.

Physically these points are said to help with the upper back, chest conditions, the heart, blood pressure and chronic conditions.

* Hold both high 19s, halfway up the arm from AP19s
* To release grief, resentment and tears, use high 19 and opposite 13

AP11 Detox

AP11 is situated halfway between the base of the neck and the top of the shoulder blade, on the trapezius muscle.

This point helps the lymph to remove all the toxins and waste from the body. As it also acts as a filter for our emotions; holding this point will help us get rid of all the emotional baggage we have accumulated ourselves and from others.

Physically it helps with the shoulders, elimination, fatigue, headaches, hormonal balance, and it detoxifies all the other points.

* Hold 11 with same side 25

AP12 Thy Will

This is found in the middle of the neck at either side of the spine. It's about surrendering into the flow of life. It helps with mental and emotional balance and also the struggles between the ego and higher intelligence.

When there is congestion on the right side, anger is expressed inwardly towards ourselves.

Congestion on the left side means our anger is expressed towards others.

Physically it is said to help with MS, fatigue, motion sickness, vertigo, the neck and also self-destructive patterns. Holding AP12 with the coccyx will help release stuck energy.

* Hold 12 with opposite 4

AP13 Love your Enemy

This point is on the chest a few inches down from the collar bone either side of the sternum.

Resentment and mistrust can get stuck here. Releasing congestion here can release us from the bondage of the past, to see the good in others and find happiness within ourselves.

Excellent for hormonal problems, fertility and tension in the neck and shoulders.

* Hold 13 and 8 together to help balance the hormones
* Or hold 13 with the opposite side 11 to help with digestion and letting go

AP14 Equilibrium

On the floating ribs below the nipple, it brings about balance and equilibrium to our whole being. It brings nourishment from assimilation not just physically but emotionally and spiritually too. It balances heaven and earth so they come together. It helps us assimilate life's experiences.

It is said to help with breathing problems, balancing the in breath and the out breath. Also, the liver, spleen and digestive organs.

* Hold 14 and opposite side 7
* Or hold both 14s with crossed hands

AP15 Joy

Situated in the groin area midway between the pubic bone and outer edge of the hip. This point is to do with joyful self-expression. It releases grief and blocked emotions, to bring joy into our lives. It helps us love and laugh and trust that the universe will bring us good things.

Said to help the libido, and good for the reproductive system, osteoporosis, prostate problems, heartache, circulation, pelvis, hips and legs.

* Hold 15 with same side 3

AP16 Foundation for Change

This is found on the outside of the ankle at the corner of the heel. This helps if we "dig our heels in" when we are reluctant to change or we are frozen due to fear. It helps release that fear of change. It supports our connection to the earth and because it relates to our muscles and skeleton, it is the foundation for all physical activities.

It can help with head and neck tension, insomnia and musculo skeletal related problems.

* Hold 16 and same side 5 for chronic pain or migraines, also for being present and grounded
* Or hold 16 with same side 12

AP17 Calm

This point is on the outside of the wrist in the hollow on the little finger side. Excellent for any nervous conditions such as anxiety, helping us let go when our minds are overactive. You can hold these points before doing something that worries you, for example when giving a presentation, exams, going somewhere new, or when you have a difficult situation to deal with.

Good for arms, ankles, fever, blood pressure, hyperactivity and hot flushes.

* Hold both 17s (this can be done by using two fingers on one point and the other thumb on the other point)

AP18 Psychologist

On the pad at the base of the thumb, AP18 governs the head. It has a balancing effect on our personality, bringing balance between being over caring or careless. It can be good for health practitioners who tend to care too much. It helps bring out an introverted or repressed personality and also calms people who can seem quite overbearing.

Can help with headaches, dizziness, insomnia, upper back, ribs and arms.

* Hold 18 with same side 4

AP19 Protection

Found in the crease of the elbow, these points improve how we interact with the world, what we put out and what we take in. They can give us protection from other people's outpourings; for example, you can hold AP19s whilst on the phone when people are telling you their problems.

AP19 can help with the arms and elbows, breast tension, digestive system and nausea.

* Hold both 19s together

High 19 is about a handspan up the arm from 19 and helps to bring calmness when facing difficult situations.

* Hold both high 19s together

AP20 Conscious Wisdom

Situated on the forehead above the centre of the eyebrows, this is where our unconscious thoughts become conscious. AP20 clears the mind, brings us logical thinking and common sense. It releases us from mental bondage and emotional stress. It allows us to know what is causing us issues.

Good for frontal headaches, sinuses and the eyes.

* Hold both 20s together
* Or hold 20 with same side 16

AP21 Clear Vision

AP21 is just under the cheekbone in line with the eyeball, it helps us see and makes sense of what we need to do. It helps our intuition and it is a very calming point too.

It can help with colds, nasal passages, sinuses, the jaw and toothache.

* Hold both 21s together
* Or hold 21 and opposite side 1

AP22 Crossroads

This is in the hollow just under the collarbone next to the sternum. This gives you more confidence in verbalising what you decide do about a problem. It allows us to assert ourselves and choose to take a step along our path. It helps us to adapt to new situations.

Good for the throat, thyroid and parathyroids, chest and digestive system.

* Hold both 22s together
* Or hold 22 with same side 3

20, 21, 22 Flow

This is a really good flow for those of us who find it hard to assert ourselves. It helps us to become clear about situations.

Also good for headaches, sinuses and sore throats.

* Hold both 20s together, then
* Hold both 21s together, then
* Hold both 22s together

AP23 Flowing with Life

This point is on the back, at the base of ribcage. It helps us with adaptability and flexibility in the flow of life. It allows us to trust in the universe so we can let go of fear. AP23 rules the adrenals and if blocked, there can be self-destructive patterns, compulsions, addictions or hyperactivity.

It is said to help with the kidneys and urinary system, adrenals, fatigue, tinnitus, chronic habits and digestion.

> ∗ Hold 23 with same side 1

As 23 can be tricky to reach on yourself, try this instead:

> ∗ Hold both high 1s together

AP24 Peace

On the outer edge of the foot midway between the toes and ankle. This helps bring harmony, peace and acceptance into your life. It brings peace out of chaos, confusion and emotional turmoil.

It's said to help energise the lymphatic system, help the feet and ankles.

> ∗ Hold 24 with opposite side 26

AP25 Regeneration

This point is on the buttocks on your sitting bone. It is a physical cleanser, releasing mental tension and toxins from mental and physical activities. It can be blocked by physical and emotional stress. AP25 helps regenerate, revitalise and rejuvenate us. Holding 25 with 8 is said to keep you young.

Helps with lower back problems, bloating, digestive system, fatigue.

> ∗ Hold 25 with opposite side 11

AP26 Completion

Found at the back of the armpit, this point harmonises everything. It brings wholeness and final completion where the past, present and future come together to complete the circle. It helps you become ready and recharged for a new beginning.

As this point will be congested if any of the other 25 are blocked, it will usually be sore.

You can hold any point with AP26 to release it.

Good for arms, upper back, chest area and for regrets.

* Hold both 26s together

Quick Releases of Blocked Points

1 with o26	**14** with o7
2 with s3	**15** with s3
3 with s15	**16** with s12
4 with o21	**17** hold both 17s
5 with s16	**18** hold both 18s
6 with s15	**19** hold both 19s
7 with s12	**20** with s16
8 with s11	**21** with o1
9 hold both 19s	**22** with s3
10 hold both high 19s	**23** both high 1s
11 with s25	**24** with o26
12 with o4	**25** with o11
13 with o11	**26** hold both 26s
s = same side o = opposite side	

When you've not got this list to hand, it's worth remembering that you can hold any point with 11 to detox and you can hold any point with 26 to clear congestion.

Major Flows

There are flows of energy around the body which when flowing freely keep us balanced, centred and in the flow of life. Think of these flows as like rivers, if the river gets blocked or constricted, this can result in stagnation in its flow. Stagnation in our energy flow means that there will be areas not receiving that energetic nourishment, which can then lead to physical problems.

To keep our energy healthy, we can use the following three flows.

Main Central Vertical Energy Flow

The Main Central Vertical Energy Flow is the deepest energy flow in the body and very beneficial for anyone who has chronic illnesses. It is great for helping the back, the spine, the spinal cord and the nervous system, the digestive system, the chakras and the meridian energies. It keeps us centred; I like to think it re aligns our whole system.

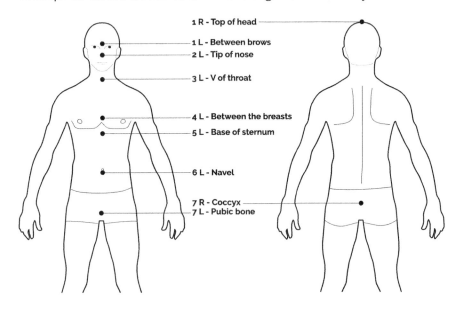

Follow the steps below:

Step 1–Right hand on top of head (crown) (Remains there until step 8)

Left middle finger on the third eye

Step 2–Left middle finger on the tip of nose

Step 3–Left middle finger in the "V" of throat

Step 4–Left middle finger on the sternum, between the breasts

Step 5–Left middle finger at the base of sternum (solar plexus)

Step 6–Left middle finger on the navel

Step 7–Left middle finger on the centre of pubic bone

Step 8–Right hand (palm side or back) on the coccyx

(Left hand stays on pubic bone)

This is a great flow to use every day, as it helps maintain health in spite of the daily stresses that surround us and deplete our energy.

How these steps can help you:

This flow harmonises all the meridian energies, whilst working on the spine, nervous system and digestive system. It helps realign your whole system.

Step 1–Is said to harmonise blood pressure, revitalise the brain, support the pineal and pituitary glands and help with sleep.

Step 2–Is said to support the pituitary gland, influence the rejuvenation and reproduction of cells and help with conception.

Step 3–Is said to support the thyroid and parathyroid glands, aid repro-duction, help with the larynx, speech, expression and creativity.

Step 4–Is said to strengthen the circulatory system, revitalise the lungs and pelvic girdle, as well as support the thymus gland.

Step 5–Is said to harmonise red and white blood cells, control secre-tions of digestive enzymes and hormones, strengthen the lymphatic system, nervous system, harmonise the spleen, adrenals, kidneys, liver, gallbladder and pancreas.

Step 6–Is said to help with breathing control, the small & large intes-tines, digestion and assimilation, and revitalise the adrenal glands.

Step 7–Is said to influence growth, the lymphatic system, reproductive glands and strengthen the spine.

Step 8–Is said to balance the reproductive organs, ureters, abdominal area, help with sciatica and the legs and feet.

When I was teaching a workshop for High Touch Acupressure, the students worked in pairs on each other. We were an odd number so I exchanged treatments with one of the students. While she was doing this flow on me, my left elbow started hurting and I couldn't find a position that was comfortable for it. I'd previously strained it carrying lots of Christmas shopping and occasionally it would flare up if I carried shopping bags for any length of time.

After the workshop, it never bothered me again!

At another class the students worked on each other using the Main Central Vertical flow. The next day, one lady said that although she hadn't thought she felt unwell or particularly unhappy before this, she had woken up that morning feeling really well, bright and very positive about the future. You can see that this flow has very positive effects on us in many different ways.

Supervisor Flows

These flows are good for clearing the head, for breathing, aiding digestion and easing back problems. They help balance the meridian flows on either side of the body. You can use these when you have a problem that is mainly on one side of the body, for instance back pain on one side.

The left flow is to do with our yin energy and the past. Related to female energy, this would help someone who is passive or withdrawn, someone who may be stuck in the past or stuck in themselves.

The right flow is to do with our yang energy and the present. Related to male energy, this would help someone who is permanently on the go, giving out too much or not taking enough in for themselves.

For problems on the left side:

* Place right hand on left side 11
* Place left hand on left side 25
* Hold together for 2–3 minutes
* Move left hand to left side 15
* Hold 11 and 15 together for 2–3 minutes

For problems on the right side:

* Place left hand on right side 11
* Place right hand on right side 25
* Hold together for 2–3 minutes
* Move right hand to right side 15
* Hold 11 and 15 together for 2–3 minutes

Diagonal Mediator Flow

Good for when you're feeling off centre, out of sorts, bumping into things, or need a change of attitude.

* Put left thumb pad onto left ring finger nail making a circle
* Place right hand over left shoulder and bring knees together so the inner sides touch, hold for 2–3 minutes or longer
* Put right thumb pad onto right ring finger nail making a circle
* Place left hand over right shoulder and bring knees together so the inner sides touch, hold for 2–3 minutes or longer

You can also use this if you have an upper and lower body problem on opposite sides, for example a right shoulder problem and a left hip/back problem.

I have seen this flow change people's attitude to situations and people, so they become much more understanding and tolerant about something that they were previously annoyed, irritable, impatient or puzzled about.

I used the diagonal mediator flow with a client who had a couple of upsetting and frustrating situations around her that she couldn't do anything about and they were causing her to feel totally overwhelmed. After using this she felt more relaxed and positive about it all, even though the problems still remained.

Simple Flows using the 26 points

As these flows are combinations of 3 points, they can be used in 2 ways:

You can choose to hold each pair of the same points together for a few minutes, then move onto the second pair and finally, onto the 3rd pair.

So, in the case of the flow 1:5:9 it would be:

* Hold both 1s together
* Hold both 5s together
* Then hold both 9s together (use 19 as a substitute for 9 on yourself)

The other way is to hold the first 2 points together on one side, then move to the 2nd and 3rd points and finally to the 3rd and 1st points all for a couple of minutes for each combination.

You would then move to the other side and repeat if necessary.

For the flow 1:5:9, it would be:

* Hold right side 1 and 5 together
* Hold right side 5 and 9 (19) together
* Hold right side 9 (19) and 1 together

Followed by:

* Hold left side 1 and 5 together
* Hold left side 5 and 9 (19) together
* Hold left side 9 (19) and 1 together

This flow helps with moving on, releasing the fear associated with it and allow change to happen. If you do the second version, this would actually take longer, so really it depends on the time you have and what your intuition tells you.

Some of these flows may do similar things but differ slightly in effects, so you can find one that fits your particular requirements at the time.

Flows that can be done both ways:

Points 1:2:9 for help with moving forward and having the energy to deal with the changes.

Points 3:6:11 to help balance breathing and the immune system, as well as detoxing.

Points 8:13:6 can help keep the hormones balanced.

Points 1:9:7 this can follow on from 1:5:9 and 1:2:9 as it helps us to move on, allow change and be victorious in what we are doing.

Points 1:10:14 for moving forward, going with the flow and assimilating the experiences.

Points 1:8:2 for the legs and lower back.

Points 1:16:25 to help us move forward without resistance, and regenerate our energy. A good physical flow for legs, feet, bones, muscles, arthritis and poor circulation.

Flows that are best done in pairs:

Points 9:10:12 this can help release all past relationships, allows us to go with the flow, so that any struggles are at an end.

* Hold both 9s (19s)
* Hold both 10s (high 19s)
* Hold both 12s

Points 9:10:7 help with releasing all past relationships, going with the flow and being victorious through this.

* Hold both 9s (19s)
* Hold both 10s (high 19s)
* Hold both 7s

Points 20:21:22 this is known as the Ladies Flow (from the days when women didn't have a voice). It helps you become clear in your mind what it is you need to do, see it clearly and state it, so it becomes actionable.

* Hold both 20s
* Hold both 21s
* Hold both 22s

Points 13:11:23 this flow is for those who take others worries on board, to help them release problems and stay in flow of life. They can then follow their destiny for themselves rather than be side-tracked by other people's problems.

* Hold both 13s
* Hold both 11s
* Hold both 23s (high 1s on yourself)

Points 23:11:10 fear can block 23, 11 to release that and 10 to let go of the past and forgive.

* Hold both 23s (high 1s on yourself)
* Hold both 11s
* Hold both 10s (high 19s on yourself)

This flow can release stiffness and inflexibility so that you can move forward in life. Physically it can be good for arthritis.

* Hold both 23s (use both high 1s on yourself)
* Hold both 11s
* Hold both 10s (high 19s)

Points 9:10:23 can help to release past relationships, go with the flow and follow your destiny without fear.

* Hold both 9s (19s)
* Hold both 10s (high 19s)
* Hold both 23s (high 1s)

Points 3:19:11 for protection against infection, protection from other people's problems, and help with detoxing from any similar past issues.

* Hold both 3s
* Hold both 19s
* Hold both 11s

Energy healing systems

I would really recommend that you learn how to use an energy healing system such as Reiki, Quantum Touch or Vortex Healing®. There are many reiki masters out there who can attune you to using reiki for yourself and for others if you wish to do so.

Although I have been attuned to reiki, I tend to use Vortex Healing® with clients in addition to reflexology, kinesiology or acupressure. I also use Vortex Healing® for distance healing with family and friends.

Quantum Touch is another energy healing system that is readily available and easy to learn and use.

The power of this was wonderfully demonstrated when I was in Bosnia[3] with a charity, helping people there who still had health problems resulting from the traumatic war in the 1990s.

Mary and I had travelled there together and she introduced me to Quantum Touch, a way of using healing energy and the breath, which she used with our Bosnian clients.

The second week we were there, the weather became very foggy and we noticed that there were no planes flying in or out of the airport, which was very near to our accommodation in Sarajevo. The day we were due to leave, Mary and I sat in the airport as our plane circled overhead, unable to land due to the heavy fog. Mary started using Quantum Touch breathing with the intention of clearing the fog. Within minutes it lifted, our plane landed, we boarded and the plane took off. We later found out that the fog had returned just after we left!

Food is your Medicine

This book is intended to help you use certain energy and other techniques that I have learned over the years from the therapies that I use and see results from, every day.

I have also mentioned other ways you can help yourself and good nutrition is definitely one of those. There are many books and articles on how food and supplements can nourish us and help improve our health and act as preventatives to disease. After all, our planet is one giant symbiotic system that has evolved over the millenniums to sustain the life upon it.

I would highly recommend that you find a good nutrition "bible" that you find easy to follow and use it to increase your understanding of how to stay healthy and full of vitality.

Having said that here are a few tasters to whet your appetite!

The Mediterranean diet has long been associated with good health and olive oil is known to keep the gut healthy, but now scientific evidence shows it can help kill off cancerous cells. Oleocanthal, the active ingredient, targets cancer cells and apparently causes die off within 30 minutes to an hour. More reasons to eat olives (I have always advocated 5 olives a day helps keep your skin soft and hydrated) and use the oil to dress your salads.

Reducing food intake fights inflammation in the body, the 5:2 diet was first introduced by Dr Michael Moseley and later he added the 16:8 diet, as a way of becoming healthier as well as for losing weight. New research[13] has shown that when calorie intake (carbohydrates especially) is restricted, this inhibits inflammatory response in the body. This means it can help with type 2 diabetes, auto-immune disorders, rheumatoid arthritis, Alzheimer's and inflammatory disorders.

Carbohydrates have had a bad press recently; however, we do need carbohydrate in our food to produce energy for the body to function.

Too much sugar and simple carbohydrates can play havoc with blood sugar levels, eventually leading to heart disease and hypertension, obesity, and diabetes.

Complex carbs are much better for us, as a rough guide that's a whole food carb–beans, sweet potato, quinoa, squash and also berries. Anything processed and refined tends to be a "baddy". These include white bread and rice, crisps, pastries and other processed foods.

Carbohydrates are involved in the production of serotonin which helps us feel good, so they calm our mood and help with stress levels. They also help with brain function; low carb dieters have been shown to score worse in memory tests.

There are a few simple things we can do to help boost our energy levels and feel better, quickly and easily. One is to drink more water and cut down on the tea and coffee. The body treats these as foods, so plain water (hot or cold) is processed better by the body. It quickly rehydrates the body's cells and helps the body deal with any toxic overload better. For good performance, clear thinking and proper body and mind function, the body depends greatly on water. Without water the body's electrical system is impaired and the lymph system and organ function suffers.

Tea, coffee and alcohol all act as stimulants to the adrenals and can contribute to extreme tiredness. Sudden fatigue and temporary confusion can be signs of dehydration, drinking plenty of water, 6–8 glasses a day can help.

Research[9] shows that people who drank 5 or more glasses of water were significantly less likely to suffer a heart attack.

Other possible risks of chronic dehydration include kidney or bladder problems, dry skin, constipation, some types of back problems and auto intoxication[8].

We know about the benefits of daily exposure to the sun for short periods to produce vitamin D in the body, if our levels of this vitamin are depleted, this can lead to fatigue. Research[14] has shown that bowel cancer patients with high levels of vitamin D are more likely to survive the disease and that it may also help prevent early death from heart disease[15].

If we can't get sunlight on our skin, then oily fish–salmon, sardines, mackerel–eggs and fortified spreads can top us up.

Another reason to get out in the fresh air and soak up some sunlight, is that looking up at the sky while we are outside has the effect of lifting our spirits (looking up prevents from accessing the part of our brain that allows us to brood on negativity) and helping us feel more positive.

Fruit and vegetables have so many beneficial properties to keep us healthy and evidence suggests we should eat a wide variety of coloured fruit and vegetables, at least 7 portions a day.

Here are some of the properties of the different coloured foods:

* Red–berries, tomatoes, contain lutein, which has been shown to help eyesight
* Orange–carrots, orange peppers, apricots, peaches and oranges have B-carotene and vitamin A for a healthy immune system and great skin
* Green–green leafy veg really help the liver and protect the digestive system
* Blue/purple–blueberries, blackberries, dark cherries and black grapes are full of anti-oxidants as well as compounds that strengthen the blood vessels

I remember going to a talk by a naturopath who said that most people rely on the same 20 foods all the time. As a family we eat lots of vegetables every day, so I assumed that we would eat many more than 20 different foods. Guess what, when I counted it up, it was 22, most were healthy options but nevertheless still only 22. If you count the different foods you and your family eat regularly, I'll bet it will be a similar number, so it's worth looking at other options. It certainly made me look again at what we eat, there are so many different types of fruit, vegetables, nuts, seeds, grains, meat and fish to choose from.

Broccoli is a superfood already known for protecting against obesity, diabetes, heart disease and cancer. A study[16] in the American Journal of Clinical Nutrition found that cruciferous vegetables like broccoli, cauliflower, cabbage and kale, may lengthen a person's lifespan.

My family know how much I love broccoli, they even had it served with pizza! They will be pleased they ate it now.

Research[17] has shown that a substance-punicalagin-in pomegranates could help people with Alzheimer's and Parkinson's. It is thought to prevent the inflammation that destroys brain cells. It is a super healthy fruit, used for centuries in folk medicine, and is claimed to be effective against many conditions, such as heart disease, high blood pressure, inflammation and even prostate cancer.

Because of our lifestyle we may be deficient in vitamins and minerals that are essential for maintaining our health. This can be due to poor diet, fast foods, the way crops are grown in nutrient poor soil, illness and other factors. There are many supplements that can support our health needs whilst we make changes to our diet, lifestyle and of course use the techniques in this book, to improve our health.

Magnesium which is in green leafy veg, fish, nuts and seeds has been shown to lower blood pressure and increase blood flow. It is also known for helping with muscle fatigue and aiding sleep; think of taking a bath with Epsom salts, your sore muscles ease and you feel sleepy afterwards.

Vitamin C and the B vitamins support our adrenals so they can help with stress.

Vitamin C and zinc support our immune system as does vitamin D.

There is much more scientific evidence coming along all the time to show that food really is our medicine.

Food intolerances

Health problems that can be associated with intolerances include digestive disorders, IBS, migraines, eczema and other skin problems, joint pain, sinusitis, hay fever and many more.

However, food intolerances are not usually a cause of these problems on their own, but a sign that the body is in overload. There is usually something underlying which is putting the body out of balance. It may be candida problems or "bad" bacteria in the gut, or the liver could be overwhelmed and just not processing stuff very efficiently.

Clients often suspect certain foods may be the problem but find that they don't always have a reaction after eating it. This is because tolerance levels can increase or decrease depending on different factors. These can be time of day, how well you're feeling, how well your day has gone and also the amount of that particular food you have eaten.

Let's take wheat for example. It may be that if you have toast for breakfast after a good night's sleep, you feel ok after, no bloating, no tiredness, no runny nose etc. If you then have a sandwich for lunch your body may protest a bit. If you follow on with pasta for tea and it's been a stressful day, then you may get all your symptoms afterwards. Yet another day you have pasta for tea after a day that has gone really well and notice very little in the way of symptoms. It can be hard to figure out if it is a wheat intolerance or not.

Many people have a test, discover they are intolerant to wheat, dairy etc, give up eating these foods and find that although it makes a difference, it's not always a huge one. This is because there are other factors involved. Helping the body get back into balance using the techniques in this book or seeing a kinesiologist, is part of the process in which the body starts to heal itself so that eventually the body doesn't react to those foods anymore. I have seen many clients re introduce foods they were previously intolerant to, back into their diet without adverse effects. When people have a test and no help to get the body healthy again, they often end up thinking they have to avoid these foods permanently, which is really quite sad.

Probiotics

Certain bacteria including *Lactobacillus* and *Bifidobacterium*, are believed to have properties which keep us healthy (anti-inflammatory, anti-tumorigenic, and pathogen exclusion properties). It is now known that having these beneficial bacteria in our gut biome can also have an effect on the way we store fat, how we balance levels of glucose in the blood, and how we respond to hormones that make us feel hungry or full.

Anxiety can cause stress within the body, using up its healthy resources and making it more prone to illness and disease. Studies[18] have shown that having the right bacteria in a healthy gut means we tend to feel happier, bad bacteria in the gut tend to create low mood and anxiety, leading to more stress and depleting the body.

Studies[19] on twins who were either both obese or lean showed that those who were lean had a much bigger variety of gut bacteria. Bacteria were then transferred into mice, those that received bacteria from the obese twins became obese themselves, whilst those receiving bacteria from the lean twins, remained lean. When they moved all the mice into the same cage, the obese ones started to lose weight as they picked up more of the "lean type" bacteria!

Next, the studies demonstrated the complex interaction among food, microbes and body weight, by feeding the mice specially prepared unhealthy food that was high in fat and low in fruits, vegetables and fibre. With this "western diet," the mice with obese-type microbes proceeded to grow fat even when housed with lean mice. The unhealthy diet somehow prevented the good bacteria from moving in and flourishing.

So having the right balance of gut bacteria is not only hugely beneficial for our health, it can help us lose weight too.

And finally

A recent study led by the Harvard T. H. Chan School of Public Health[20] showed that these 5 excellent habits during adulthood may add more than a decade to life expectancy:

* Healthy diet
* Regular exercise
* Keeping a healthy body weight
* Not drinking too much alcohol
* Not smoking

I will add one more, use the fast fixes in this book—regularly!

I wish you a long and happy, healthy life

References

Much of the material for this book has come from techniques I have learned and adapted from the many courses I have taken and books I have read, on Reflexology, Kinesiology and High Touch Acupressure.

Essential Kinesiology Techniques for Muscle Testing Practitioners, by Terry Larder

Accurate muscle testing for food and supplements plus Balancing Meridians, by Elizabeth Barhydt and Hamilton Barhydt

High Touch Jin Shin Workbooks I & II by Betsy Ruth Dayton

The Touch of Healing by Alice Burmeister with Tom Monte

Numbered references in this book:

1 https://www.sciencedaily.com/
releases/2015/06/150608081753.htm

2 https://www.healthcmi.com/Acupuncture-Continuing-Education-News/1230-new-ct-scans-reveal-acupuncture-points

3 https://www.lindahoyland.com/my-experiences-of-bosnia/

4 https://www.bachcentre.com/

5 https://feinstein.northwell.edu/institutes-researchers/
our-researchers/kevin-j-tracey-md

6 https://www.psychologytoday.com/gb/blog/
the-athletes-way/201405/how-does-the-vagus-nerve-convey-gut-instincts-the-brain

7 https://www.heart.org/en/healthy-living/fitness/fitness-basics/staying-hydrated-staying-healthy

8 https://www.medicalnewstoday.com/articles/290814

9 https://www.npr.org/sections/health-shots/2015/09/01/436385137/

10 https://theconversation.com/how-do-our-brains-reconstruct-the-visual-world-49276

11 https://www.nhs.uk/news/lifestyle-and-exercise/back-pain-leading-cause-of-disability-study-finds/

12 https://www.bbc.co.uk/news/health-43674270

13 https://www.livescience.com/55425-calorie-restriction-inflammation.html

14 https://www.medicalnewstoday.com/articles/324984

15 https://www.sciencedaily.com/releases/2015/11/151109160556.htm

16 https://www.soundhealthandlastingwealth.com/health-news/how-to-live-longer-eating-more-of-this-type-of-vegetable-could-boost-life-expectancy/

17 https://www.sciencedaily.com/releases/2014/08/140822094106.htm

18 https://www.discovermagazine.com/mind/gut-bacterias-role-in-anxiety-and-depression-its-not-just-in-your-head

19 Science, Vol 341, Issue 6150

20 https://www.sciencedaily.com/releases/2018/04/180430075619.htm

Acknowledgements

Many thanks to my family and friends for their help and support.

To Jan Dixon, who helped edit and proof read this book. To Mandi Allen and Lynnda Worsnop for their writing support and help with marketing.

Thank you also to Terry Larder, Maureen Foers and Michaela Davis for their generous reviews.

And a huge thanks to my very talented son Matthew Bentley who did all of the artwork and for his patience with all the tweaking....

Printed in Great Britain
by Amazon

47139785R00119